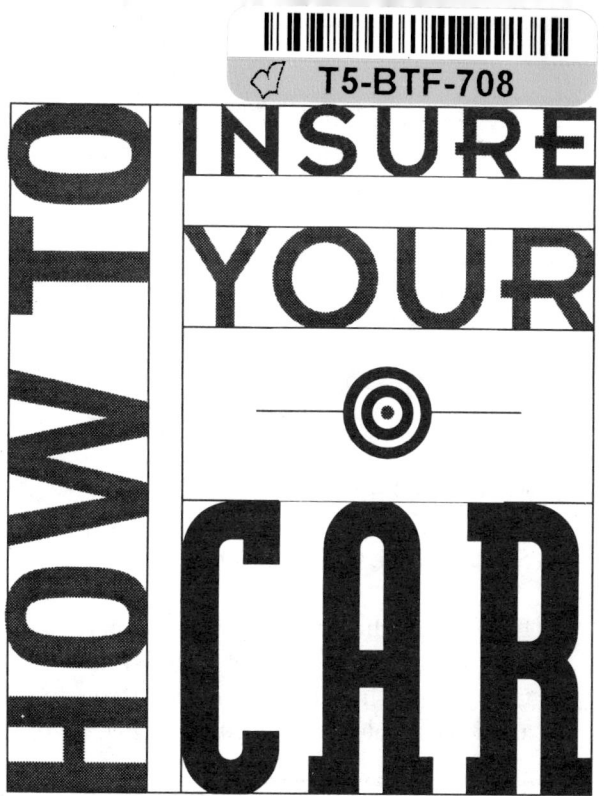

HOW TO INSURE YOUR CAR

A Step by Step Guide to Buying the Coverage You Need at Prices You Can Afford

THE MERRITT EDITORS

MERRITT PUBLISHING
A DIVISION OF THE MERRITT COMPANY
SANTA MONICA, CALIFORNIA

How to Insure Your Car

First edition, 1996
Copyright © 1996 by Merritt Publishing

Merritt Publishing
1661 Ninth Street
Santa Monica, California 90406

For a list of other publications or for more information, please call (800) 638-7597. Outside the United States and in Alaska and Hawaii, please call (310) 450-7234.

All rights reserved. No part of this book may be reproduced, stored in a retrieval system or transcribed in form or by any means (electronic, mechanical, photocopy, recording or otherwise) without the prior written permission of Merritt Publishing.

Library of Congress Catalogue Number: 96-079504

The Merritt Editors
How to Insure Your Car
Includes index.
Pages: 265

ISBN: 1-56343-117-4
Printed in the United States of America.

ACKNOWLEDGMENTS

The Merritt Editors who contributed to this book include Debora Chan, Cynthia Davidson, John Hartnett, Jan King and James Walsh. Thanks to Mimi Tennant and Wendy Heichman for helping polish the final product. Thanks also to: Kimberly Baer Design Associates, Kathie Baumoel, Cynthia Chaillie, Ginger McKelvey and Megan Thorpe.

Some forms that appear in this book are based on standard forms used with the permission of the Insurance Services Office.

How to Insure Your Car is the first book in Merritt Publishing's *How to Insure...* series. Upcoming titles will include *How to Insure Your Life* and *How to Insure Your Home*. Because these books are designed to make the concepts and theories of insurance understandable to ordinary consumers, the Merritt Editors welcome any feedback. Please fax at (310) 396-4563 or call (800) 638-7597 during ordinary business hours, Pacific time. More information from Merritt Publishing is available on the InsWeb Internet site at http://www.insweb.com.

TABLE OF CONTENTS

CHAPTER 1
Why You Need Car Insurance — 1

CHAPTER 2
How to Figure Out How Much
Car Insurance You Need — 21

CHAPTER 3
How Car Insurance Works — 47

CHAPTER 4
Important Definitions — 69

CHAPTER 5
Why Liability Is an Important
Issue — 89

CHAPTER 6
Why Uninsured Motorists Coverage
Is Important — 103

CHAPTER 7
How No-Fault Insurance Works — 117

TABLE OF CONTENTS

CHAPTER 8
How Endorsements and Other
Changes Work   **131**

CHAPTER 9
Tips for Shopping for Car
Insurance   **145**

CHAPTER 10
How Insurance Companies
Price Coverage   **171**

CHAPTER 11
How to Make an Insurance Claim   **193**

CHAPTER 12
Common Problems—And How
to Avoid Them   **215**

CHAPTER 13
Fraud   **239**

INDEX   **255**

CHAPTER 1

WHY YOU NEED CAR INSURANCE

Dan Charron found an old-fashioned way to handle the high price of car insurance. The Ontario, Canada, driver—who didn't have any accidents on his driving record—was so frustrated with the cost of auto insurance that he got rid of his car and started riding a horse to work.

"It's more a protest to the insurance business," Charron told a local newspaper in early 1995. "It is humorous, but I'm speaking for a lot of people."

He figured he'd save about $17,000 over five years by not paying car insurance premiums.

Riding a horse isn't an option for most people. In most states you **have to buy auto insurance** if you drive a car.

> Insurance is a necessity if you drive a car or use a commercial lender to finance your automobile purchase. And annual premiums can amount to a considerable amount of money. So doing the research is worthwhile.

NECESSARY COVERAGES

Bodily injury liability. If you injure someone in a car accident, this coverage pays their medical and rehabilitation expenses and any damages for which they may sue you. In most states, you must buy coverage of at least $15,000/$30,000 (the $15,000 pays for injuries to one person; the $30,000 is the total available per accident).

Property damage liability. If you damage someone's property in an accident for which you are at fault, this coverage pays to fix it. In most states, you must buy $5,000 worth of coverage. Many standard policies include a higher limit—often $25,000.

Medical benefits. This coverage pays medical bills for you and others covered on your policy, no matter who was at fault for the accident. In most states, you must buy at least $5,000 worth of coverage. The typical driver buys $10,000 worth. This coverage usually does not have a deductible.

ALMOST NECESSARY COVERAGES

Collision. This coverage pays to repair damage to your car in an accident. Like medical benefits, it's no-fault coverage. If you're financing a car purchase, most lenders require you to buy collision coverage. Insurance companies will usually give you a $500 deductible unless you request another amount. The higher your deductible, the lower your premium.

Comprehensive. This coverage pays for theft or damage to your car from hazards including fire, flood, vandalism or striking an animal. Again, most lenders require you to buy this coverage if you're financing your car. And you can also set your deductible for this coverage.

Uninsured/underinsured motorist. This coverage pays for losses and damages, including your medical bills, lost wages and pain and suffering, if you are hit by a person who doesn't have any insurance or enough to cover the damage. It usually makes sense to purchase the same level of this coverage that you have for bodily injury liability.

OPTIONAL COVERAGES

Extraordinary medical benefits. This coverage pays when your medical and rehabilitation expenses exceed the limits in your policy. It provides $1 million of coverage.

Income loss. This coverage pays the amount of your take-home pay when injuries from an accident keep you from working. Payments are made without regard to whether you have other disability insurance coverage.

Funeral benefit. This coverage pays up to $2,500 if you or a family member dies in an auto accident. The cost is nominal. Nationwide, for instance, charges 40 cents per year for $1,500 worth of coverage.

Rental car replacement. This coverage pays a set amount per day for a rental car if your car is being repaired because of an accident.

Towing and labor costs. This coverage pays for road service, such as jump-starting your car or changing a flat tire, and towing, which can be used anytime your car breaks down, not just when it's involved in an accident. The coverage shouldn't cost very much—usually less than $5 a year.

CHANGES TO THE SYSTEM

The way insurance is structured and sold is going through some **significant changes**. Before the 1980s, the question most people asked themselves was: Can I afford the car I really want? Since the 1980s, the question has become: Okay, I can—just barely—afford the car...but can I afford to carry insurance on it?

Insurance companies decide to whom they'll sell a policy as well as the price they'll charge—virtually different for every person—based on a two-page application form. Knowing how to fill out that application becomes a critical process.

> Knowing how insurance companies will use the information you give them puts you on even footing. Knowing what kind of insurance you need—and what you don't—can give you an edge.

IT'S ABOUT MONEY AND RISK

According to the Washington, D.C.-based group Consumers Union, the average household spends $9,000 over a 10-year period on auto insurance, but files just one claim—typically for about $600. That sounds like

CHAPTER 1

a bad deal. But, if you know what you're doing, you can make it better.

Auto insurance remains controversial because it's influenced by behavioral and demographic realities that some people would rather avoid. But avoiding reality is silly. And it can be expensive.

Consider these California Highway Patrol figures for 1989:

- The 20-to-24 age group accounted for 10.6 percent of all drivers. They were involved in 17.6 percent of the fatal accidents and 16.6 percent of the injury accidents.

- The 60-to-64 age group accounted for 4.9 percent of all drivers. They were involved in 2.9 percent of the fatal accidents and 2.6. percent of the injury accidents.

- The over-65 age group represented 11.2 percent of the state's licensed drivers. They were involved in 7.3 percent of the fatal accidents and 5.6 percent of the injury accidents.

A National Highway Traffic Safety Administration report found the nationwide **crash involvement rate** for the 16-to-19 age group is 28.6 accidents per million **vehicle miles traveled**. The rates drop markedly for the middle-age brackets; then they rise again in the senior range, reaching 6.4 for the 70-to-74 age group and 7.7 for the 75-to-79. Among the oldest drivers, the crash rates reach their highest levels—15.1 for the 80-to-84 group and 38.8 at ages 85 and older.

WHY YOU NEED CAR INSURANCE

Of course, auto insurance can't prevent automobile accidents from happening. Its purpose is to **offset some of the financial loss** that results from an accident. This kind of financial protection is generally referred to as coverage.

> The key to buying the right kind of auto insurance and using it cost-effectively once you've bought it is understanding how the coverage works.

As you'll see in this book, various coverages are designed to protect your **auto investment**, to pay **medical expenses** when injury occurs, and to cover your legal **liability** to others who may suffer injury or damages.

This doesn't mean that all possible expenses or losses will be covered. **Limits** of insurance apply to insurance coverages, and each insurance policy has exclusions and exceptions.

Still, auto insurance is designed to reduce many of the financial losses that could otherwise result from owning or operating a car. Without insurance, you would have to bear the entire cost when accidental injuries or damages occur.

THE RULES OF THE INSURANCE GAME

The changes that are working through the insurance industry affect you—as an auto insurance **policyholder**—in a couple of basic ways.

CHAPTER 1

First, **the way insurance is sold** is changing. It used to be sold exclusively through middlemen—the insurance agents—who either represented one company or a group of companies. In the 1990s, a growing number of auto insurance companies have switched to selling insurance **directly** to policyholders. They do this through direct mail, telephone marketing and even computer on-line services.

If you use an insurance agent, that person makes a 15 percent commission when you buy your auto insurance policy and an additional 12 to 15 percent each time you renew it. This commission can be a good investment if your situation is unusual or if you expect difficulties making claims. But, for many people, that money would be better spent buying **additional coverage**.

Second, the way in which states **regulate the sale** and use of insurance is changing. Most states have specific requirements for auto coverage, and many insurance companies offer basic coverage that fulfills those requirements.

State insurance regulators watch auto coverage closely. They focus on two areas: **rate setting** and **claims paying**. Auto insurance companies have a reputation—in some cases, well-deserved—for being very slow to pay even legitimate claims.

According to one survey conducted in Washington state, more than 40 percent of those who filed auto insurance claims are not completely satisfied with the results. Other states find even more people unhappy.

Claims handling represents the number one auto insurance complaint that most state insurance commissioners report. Widespread poor experiences contribute to the consumer's distrust of insurance companies and the way they do business.

Third, the **role of insurance** in society is changing. As more people grow more wealthy—even if it's just relatively wealthy—they have more to protect. This makes insurance less of an optional safety measure and more of a necessity of life.

> All of these changes make it more important that you understand the fundamentals of how the coverage works.

WHAT YOU'LL FIND IN THIS BOOK

The purpose of this book is to help you understand:

- how insurance works,
- why certain kinds of insurance are important,
- how to calculate your needs,
- how to buy insurance wisely,
- how to read the policy you buy,
- how insurance is priced,
- how to make a claim when you need to,
- how to avoid common claims problems, and

- how to avoid getting ripped off.

You'll find these points handled in each chapter, offering background **explanations, examples, case study illustrations, checklists** and **sample forms**.

BUYING INSURANCE BECAUSE YOU HAVE TO

The main reason you need car insurance is that the law says you have to have it. This **mandated insurance** usually relates to liability exposures. You have to be able to pay for damage to other people or their property that you cause.

Most states call these laws **financial responsibility** requirements. Technically, you can use something other than insurance to meet the requirements. Many states will allow you to post a cash bond instead of buying insurance. If you cause an accident, anyone you hurt can make a claim against the bond.

But, for most people, insurance is the most cost-effective way to meet the responsibility requirements.

Each state has its own specific laws regarding **financial responsibility**, insurance coverage, or **no-fault coverage**.

The variations that exist from state to state can cause some confusion. The standard car insurance policy[1] issued by the Insurance Services Office (ISO)—a clearing house for insurance industry information—includes the following language:

---

[1] While each state makes specific changes for its insurance requirements, the ISO standard policy remains a **common** reference point that all states use. Throughout this book, we will refer to the ISO standard auto policy form when discussing policy language.

> When this policy is certified as future proof of financial responsibility, this policy shall comply with the law to the extent required.

A state may require evidence of financial responsibility from a driver in order to reinstate a driver's license which has been suspended or revoked due to a bad driving record or an unsatisfied judgment from a previous auto accident. One means of showing proof is for the insurance carrier to file a document with the state agency certifying coverage in force, policy limits, coverage dates, etc.

OTHER KINDS OF MANDATED COVERAGE

If you've borrowed money to buy a car, the **lending institution** will usually insist that you have collision coverage. If you don't—or the insurance you have lapses while you still owe money on the car—the finance company may buy insurance for you and add the cost to the money you owe. This **replacement insurance** is usually extremely expensive and extremely limited in what it covers.

> The whole issue of forced replacement insurance is controversial.

In January 1995, a $38.5 million jury decision against Mississippi banking company Trustmark Corp. brought the practice of replacement insurance into question.

# CHAPTER 1

A Mississippi jury awarded the surprisingly large amount to a man and his father-in-law, concluding that the bank had wrongly billed them $9,000 for what it called collateral protection insurance. The premiums, which Trustmark added to the amount owed on the car, were more than the 1988 Nissan Sentra itself.

The car was eventually repossessed because the owner couldn't make payments on the $9,000 premiums. The former owner then sued.

Lawrence Abernathy, the lawyer who represented the owner of the Nissan and his father-in-law, said he had some 20 other lawsuits pending against Trustmark concerning its auto insurance financing practices. He has also requested class-action status for the cases, in response to the prospect of an increased case load.

COVERAGE FOR DAMAGE TO YOUR AUTO

Even though you have to have insurance when you drive a car, most people want to buy insurance to protect their automotive investment.

The standard Personal Auto Policy provides coverage for **damages to covered autos**. Although it is called "Coverage for Damage to Your Auto" in the policy, it has traditionally been known as physical damage coverage.

This part of the policy says that the insurance company will "pay for direct and accidental loss to your covered auto, or any non-owned auto, including its equipment, minus any applicable deductible." It therefore covers any type of damage which is not excluded.

WHY YOU NEED CAR INSURANCE

If the collision damages more than one "covered auto," the highest applicable deductible will apply.

Coverage for Damage to Your Auto actually consists of two separate coverages—"collision" and "other than collision." You can buy **either or both** of these coverages for each car you insure. Each coverage applies only when the Declarations indicate that the coverage is provided by showing a premium for the vehicle.

In the standard auto policy, "collision" is defined as "the upset of your covered auto or a non-owned auto or their impact with another vehicle or object." Note that **collision with an object** is covered, even if it is not another vehicle.

The standard policy clearly spells out the losses that are **not collision losses** ("Other than Collision Coverage"): missiles, falling objects, fire, theft, explosion, earthquake, windstorm, hail, water, flood, malicious mischief, vandalism, riot, civil commotion, contact with a bird or animal, and breakage of glass.

Auto policies are almost always written with **higher deductibles** for collision than for non-collision losses.

> Deductibles are an amount of money you have to pay before your insurance takes over. In auto insurance, deductibles usually fall in the range between $250 and $1,000 per loss. If you have a $500 deductible and get in an accident that does $2,000 in damage to the front end of your car, you have to pay the first $500 and the insurance company will pay the $1,500 balance.

CHAPTER 1

By treating contact with an animal as a non-collision loss, you have the advantage of having a lower deductible[2] apply. This difference in deductibles is an implicit recognition of the fact that drivers usually have greater opportunities to avoid contact with other cars or objects than free-moving creatures that react unpredictably to lights, motion, and sound.

If you cause an accident that results in damage to a **car you're driving but don't own**, the ISO standard policy will provide the broadest coverage applicable to any covered auto.

> The standard policy defines "non-owned auto" as any private passenger auto, pickup, van, or trailer which is operated by or in the custody of, but is not owned by or furnished for the regular use of, the named insured or a family member. Also included is coverage for "temporary substitute automobiles."

TRAVEL

Drivers often take their cars into a state other than the one in which they live. Because insurance laws vary from state to state, settling a claim can become complicated if an accident occurs when you are away from your home state.

The **out-of-state coverage** provisions in a standard auto policy refer not only to the required minimum amounts of coverage, but to required types of cover-

---

[2] For more on deductibles, how they work and how they impact the cost of insurance, see Chapter 9.

age as well. This means that if you drive into a state where no-fault benefits or other types of coverage are required, the policy will automatically provide the minimum amounts and types of coverage.

> Most personal auto policies restrict the policy territory to the United States, its territories and possessions, Puerto Rico, and Canada.

If you are traveling outside your home state, the policy will adjust to these laws by automatically increasing the liability limits to conform to that state's laws, and providing coverages as required by the state to conform to its laws with respect to a nonresident driving in the state.

> If you drive your car into Mexico you must have valid liability insurance from a Mexican insurer. If you do not and are involved in an accident in Mexico, you may be detained in jail, have your car impounded, and be subject to other penalties.

CAR RENTALS

One of the most frequently-asked questions about car insurance is: Do I need to buy insurance when I rent a car?

CHAPTER 1

When you rent a car, you will usually be offered a **collision damage waiver** or CDW. (Some rental companies use the term **loss damage waiver** or LDW—the coverage is effectively the same.)

This waiver releases you from responsibility for damage to the rental car, provided you comply with the rental contract terms. If you decline the coverage and have an accident, you may be held responsible for the entire value of the car.

One common problem is that many of these policies contain **limitations and loopholes** that renters can unwittingly violate, voiding the coverage. For example, CDW can be voided if you drive on an unpaved road...or if you engage in "negligent" driving—and the car-rental company defines negligent.

> CDW is usually overpriced, adding about $11 a day to the cost of renting a car in 1995. In Illinois and New York—two states where rental companies have to bundle collision coverage into the advertised rental rate—average rates are only about $2.50 a day higher than in the rest of the country.

CDW often duplicates coverage you already have. Many regular auto insurance policies cover damage to rented cars, although the fine print may restrict the types of rentals it covers.

Before you turn down the rental coverage, though, it's important to know what kind of coverage you already have.

If you carry collision insurance on your own car and your policy also covers rented—technically called **non-owned**—vehicles, it is safe to decline the collision damage waiver.

As for liability insurance, your own auto policy should protect you and your passengers in a rented car as well as in your own car.

For example, if a rental car is stolen from you, the loss of the vehicle itself might be covered as a theft loss under your policy. But the insuring agreement for physical damage losses only applies to **direct loss**. If it takes some time for the insurance company to settle the claim, the rental car company might incur additional losses because the car is not available to earn rental income by renting it to someone else. This would be a **loss of use expense** for the rental car company. Whether the insured is legally liable for this loss might depend upon the circumstances of the theft and the content of the rental car agreement you've signed.

Coverage may also depend on whether you use the car for **business or pleasure** or whether your vehicle at home is still being used in your absence. Some policies limit the number of **rental days** covered each year. Others apply **deductibles and lower liability limits** to collision coverage—and therefore rental car coverage.

CDW isn't the only additional insurance rental companies may try to sell you. Other kinds include:

- Supplemental liability insurance. Unlike the CDW/LDW, this option protects the renter against property-damage or personal-injury claims over and above basic liability limits provided in the rental agreement—usually the minimum required by state law.

- Personal-effects coverage. This provides limited reimbursement to the renter for loss of baggage and other personal property during the rental period.

- Personal accident insurance. This provides limited accidental-death benefits for the renter and—often—passengers.

Of these, **supplemental liability** is one coverage you should consider—depending on where you're renting the car. In some states, major car rental companies are beginning to shift **primary liability** responsibility to renters who have personal insurance. That means without supplementary coverage you could be faced with financial disaster if you are sued.

Your own auto insurance will cover collision damage to the car you rent. It also probably covers you for liability in case you hurt someone or damage someone else's property. Your homeowner's or occupant's household policy may well cover your personal effects, even when you're on a trip.

> If you need extra accident insurance, you need it full time, not just in a rented car.

LOST WAGES

Another reason that some people buy car insurance is to provide coverage for **lost wages** that might occur after an accident. This kind of coverage is often called an **income continuation benefit**. Policies that offer this benefit cover some portion of salary and other wages you don't receive while recuperating from injuries suffered in a car accident. But these losses are sometimes difficult to establish.

The most common issue: People try to make claims for **loss of future earnings** when they are seriously disabled in a car accident. These claims seek money for income that might have been earned in the future—and they happen more often than you might think. People hurt while riding in someone else's car, people driving their own cars and even the families of people killed in car accidents have tried to make future earnings claims.

In most cases, courts have ruled that lost wages are covered only during a period of recuperation from injuries suffered in an accident. So, it's not an indefinite benefit.

Laws restricting lost wages coverage are now common throughout the country. Although the statutory language varies somewhat from state to state, the prevailing rule is that wage continuation benefits, when characterized in the statute as being in the nature of disability benefits, are **not required to be paid for periods after the insured person's death.**

CONCLUSION

This chapter has explored some of the most basic reasons that you need to have auto insurance. In the next chapter, we'll look at some of the tools you can use to calculate exactly how much—and what kind—of car insurance you should buy.

WHY YOU NEED CAR INSURANCE

CHAPTER 2

HOW TO FIGURE OUT HOW MUCH CAR INSURANCE YOU NEED

Once you've determined whether or not you need car insurance at all, your next step is to determine what kind of coverage—and how much—you need to buy.

As an auto insurance policyholder, your choice of which coverage to purchase will be influenced by the following **questions**:

- What coverage must be purchased because of state law?
- Which coverage do you need or want?
- How much will optional coverages cost (the more coverages being purchased, the higher the premium)?

WHO YOU ARE

This is the most important factor in determining your insurance needs. It's not a philosophical question—but a simpler matter of calculating what kind of **risk profile** you pose to an insurance company. Some elements of this profile are based on **demographic factors** beyond your control. Other elements are based on **lifestyle needs** that you can identify—and even change, if you choose to.

Certain **age, sex** and **marital status** classifications are what insurance companies refer to as **primary factors** figured into premium formulas.

The age classifications usually apply to youthful operators. Among youthful operators, greater distinctions have been made in the risk factors attributable to age, sex, marital status, driver training credit, and whether an operator is a good student.

> If you're a young driver insuring yourself, you'll pay more than any other age group. Depending on where you live, you may have very few choices about what kind of insurance you can buy. If you're a parent or guardian who has a young driver in your family, he or she will likely be the single biggest cost driver in your insurance premium. If the young driver qualifies, inquire about good student discounts.

Within the age brackets, gender and marital status take effect. For example, all males under age 25 qualify as youthful operators with most insurance companies—but only unmarried females automatically do. Generally, single men younger than 25 will pay the highest premiums.

As dated a concept as it may seem, marital status does mean a great deal to insurance companies. Most insurance companies say that married people are less likely to be involved in car accidents. So, when you're calculating your needs, being married probably adds another driver to your policy—but it moves you into a better risk profile.

For adult operators, there are only three classifications based on age and sex—all other classifications relate to use of the vehicle. However, on the other end of the lifespan from the youthful operator, senior citizens are the main adult classification. Older drivers pay more for less insurance.

> Senior citizens can usually get discounts if they successfully take driver safety courses. Also, their discounts for keeping various lines of insurance—for instance, homeowners and personal liability—with the same company are sometimes bigger.

Periodically, demographic premium ratings are challenged in court. The often-cited 1983 Florida appeals court decision *State Department of Insurance v. Insurance Services Office* defended the practice of using demographic factors in determining how much insurance a person can buy at what price.

The decision overturned a rule prohibiting insurers from, "with respect to premiums charged for automobile insurance, unfairly discriminating solely on the basis of age, sex, marital status, or scholastic achievement."

The Florida court held that the rule was an invalid exercise of delegated authority. It reasoned:

> In enacting this statute the legislature obviously intended to permit discrimination based on sex, marital status, and scholastic achievement so long as this discrimination is not unfair or based solely on these factors.

YOUR DRIVING RECORD

While who you are is the primary factor that influences how insurance companies look at you as an auto risk, there are **secondary rating factors** based on some specific variables unique to each individual. These secondary factors also determine your coverage needs.

Your **driving record** (what insurance companies call sub-class) is the most important of these secondary factors. Insurance company statistics say that, the more accidents you have, the more likely you will be involved in another accident.

If someone in your family has a bad driving record, you need to consider two things. First, you may be limited in what kind of insurance you can buy. Second, you may have different needs than you thought you did. While a high-risk driver increases your insurance costs, he or she also increases your need for liability, medical payments, collision and other than collision coverages.

THE VEHICLES IN YOUR HOUSEHOLD

The drivers in your household and their driving records

	make	model	year	VIN
Vehicle 1				
Vehicle 2				
Vehicle 3				
Vehicle 4				

	name	age	moving violations last 5 yrs.	at-fault accidents last 5 yrs.	primary vehicle
Driver 1 (named insured)					
Driver 2					
Driver 3					
Driver 4					
Driver 5					

Age impacts your insurance costs on the low and high ends—under 24 years and over 65 years will make coverage more expensive. You may have to adjust liability limits accordingly.

List moving violations by charge (speeding, reckless driving, driving while intoxicated). If a driver has had several violations, check his or her license status.

List damages related to at-fault accidents, if that information is available.

The primary vehicle column refers to any household vehicles this person drives more than anyone else does. A vehicle driven primarily by a high-risk driver—i.e., a teenager—will cost more to insure than a vehicle driven occasionally by that driver.

At some point, you may need to take the keys away from a risky driver. In the insurance context, you can do this by making that person a named exclusion from coverage under your policy. Be careful of doing this—it's a dire situation. The insurance company will write this kind of exclusion, but it may leave you effectively self-insuring that high-risk driver. If you exclude him or her by name from your coverage, make sure that person doesn't drive.

> In practical terms, excluding family members from an insurance policy doesn't work very often. It doesn't solve your problem—only the insurance company's. When this does work, it usually involves older family members whose driving skills have been eroded by age. Exclude a teenager only if you're certain you can keep him or her from driving.

WHERE YOU LIVE—WITHIN THE STATE

Another factor is what kind of **neighborhood** you live in. If you live in a large metropolitan area, you will probably pay more for auto insurance. If you live in certain zip codes or areas within a big city, your insurance may be even more expensive still.

While some insurance reform plans do away with it, most states still allow insurance companies to adjust insurance rates according to neighborhood. This practice—in extreme cases, called **red-lining**—penalizes people who live in high-crime and high-accident areas. Critics argue that this quickly becomes a mechanism for unfairly discriminating against certain groups of people.

> Candid insurance companies admit this is a process of discriminating bad risks from good ones. They argue that claims histories support their premium structures.

For your insurance needs, higher local rates mean more people may be driving without insurance. They also mean a greater risk of hit-and-run accidents. That means **uninsured and underinsured motorists** coverage becomes more important. If you live in a big city and drive a new car, you should make sure you have UM that covers the car's value—and your own.

In most states, UM applies only to **bodily injury**. In a few states, it also applies to **property damage**, or property damage UM coverage may be available as an optional coverage. Rates for UM coverage often apply to $50,000 single limit coverage or $25,000/50,000 split limits of coverage. If higher limits are desired, an additional flat-dollar premium charge is added to the base rate.

Also, living in a high-risk neighborhood puts more importance on keeping your car in a **garage**. Garaged cars are less likely to be sideswiped by errant drivers or stolen. If you keep your car inside, you'll get a break on your insurance premium. In a high-risk area, that break will be bigger.

HOW MANY ASSETS DO YOU HAVE TO PROTECT?

You probably can't change the demographics of your life. But that's only part of calculating your needs. A lot of what determines how much insurance you should buy is based on things you have more control over.

First, your **net worth** defines how much liability coverage you should buy. If you're not worth much, the state minimums will probably cover any liability you might face. But, if you have some equity worth protecting, you'll want to make sure you're covered on the liability end.

> They usually don't realize it, but driving is the most potentially dangerous thing most people do in the normal course of their lives. In terms of financial liability, a two-car accident involving four people can easily generate several million dollars in losses.

You don't have to be rich to be concerned about **protecting your assets**. In states with a liability minimum of $50,000, even the equity in a modest suburban house is worth protecting with a higher liability limit. That's why most companies offer standard insurance packages that include $100,000, $300,000 and even $1 million in liability coverage.

One simple way to calculate how much liability coverage you need is to add up the **equity value** you have in your house, any other property you own, major personal possessions like cars, jewelry or collectibles and any savings or liquid investments you have. (In the cases of the real estate and possessions, you don't even have to own them outright. Calculate the current market value minus whatever debts you have against that value.)

PERSONAL ASSETS INVENTORY

	market value	related debt and restrictions	net value
1. home			
2. other real estate			
3. capital investments			
4. cash savings			
5. accessible pension accounts			
6. cars, other vehicles			
7. art, other collectibles			
8. jewelry, etc.			
9. recreational equipment			
10. other items			
total			

> List most recent comparable value or insured value from other coverages for market value.
>
> Debts and restrictions include mortgages, liens and other encumbrances on real estate property. They would also include margin loans on capital investments and liquidations costs or penalties on accessible pension accounts.
>
> The market value applicable to cars and other vehicles should be consistent with the insured values listed elsewhere in your auto policy.
>
> Art, jewelry and other collectibles may be covered separately under a homeowners insurance policy. If so, you may choose to keep them out of this calculation. However, some homeowners policies limit coverage for auto-related liabilities. If you have a substantial amount of money tied up in these kinds of possessions, you should consider umbrella liability coverage.

The total value of all these things—even if you couldn't raise it by selling everything tomorrow—is what you need to protect. You should have liability coverage of at least this amount.

> The biggest mistake most people make on their auto insurance is that they are underinsured on liability coverage and overinsured on collision and comprehensive coverage.

Some experts advise you to add in any **pension or retirement benefits** you have or investments you've made. Although these usually can't be seized or liquidated in a legal judgment, their benefits can be attached over time. To be conservative, you might want liability coverage equal to your retirement benefit.

If you have assets worth more than $300,000, you should consider buying a $1 million liability **umbrella policy** in addition to your auto insurance. An umbrella policy covers everything and pays off if damages exceed the limits of either your auto or homeowners policies. A $1 million umbrella policy generally costs $100 to $200 a year.

Liability coverage isn't the only part of the auto insurance package that you can adjust. The **medical payments** section can also include greater or lesser levels of coverage. Medical payments coverage is always written with a **single basic limit** that applies per person in each accident—but that limit can be adjusted.

You can increase the amount of medical payments coverage above basic limits. In most cases, this is an easier process than increasing liability limits. You simply add a flat dollar amount to the published rate for each additional unit (usually $5,000) of coverage.

> Generally, if you have a health insurance plan for you and your family with which you're happy, you can keep the medical payments coverage to the state minimum.

In some cases, your insurance company or agent—if you use one—might say that **higher liability limits and lower medical payments limits** are tough to combine. Don't take this as an absolute. While some insurance companies prefer to keep liability limits consistent in high, middle and low packages, they can mix coverage levels.

HOW YOU USE YOUR CAR

Your insurance needs and the insurance company's risk analysis coincide in the question of how you use your car or cars. The insurance company's primary rating factors include **automobile use classifications**. These include "pleasure use," "business use," "farm use," and "driving to work."

If you only use the car for **pleasure** (this is sometimes called **occasional use**), your premium will be lower than if you drive it every day to **work**. Cars that you claim for **business use** tend to be even more expensive to insure.

Generally, the use issue comes into play when you're insuring **more than one car.** If your household has two or three cars, you probably shouldn't insure them all as work- or business-related. Try to insure at least one of the cars you don't drive everyday as pleasure or occasional use.

> Let your insurance company know when you won't be using your car for a long period of time—more than thirty days. You might be able to cancel your collision costs while you're gone.

Obviously, the number of cars you have also impacts the kind of insurance you buy. A Personal Auto Policy will either be rated as a single car risk or a multi-car risk. In most cases, the multi-car risk will be more cost-effective than insuring cars separately. But this issue is worth exploring with your insurance company or agent—especially if you have a high-risk driver in your household.

THE MAKE, MODEL AND AGE OF YOUR CAR

The final—and, to some people, the most important—risk factor that impacts what kind of insurance you need is what kind of car or cars you're insuring. More specifically, this factor considers the **make, model and age** of your car.

CRITICAL INFORMATION RELATING TO VEHICLES IN YOUR HOUSEHOLD

	make	model	year	VIN	model number	license number	date purchased	insured value
Vehicle 1								
Vehicle 2								
Vehicle 3								
Vehicle 4								

Almost all of this information should be available from your state vehicle registration, title or financing contract—if you have one. You have some discretion in setting the insured value, but in most cases it will be the "blue book" industry standard value for used cars.

HOW TO FIGURE OUT HOW MUCH CAR INSURANCE YOU NEED

In most cases, the older a car, the less insurance you need. This is because the **replacement value** diminishes with age.

In the case of collectible or antique cars, you can opt to insure a pre-determined replacement value. Insurance companies usually offer this in the form of a premium per $100 of **declared value**.

For example, a 1956 Chevy in mint condition would be worth far more than another 1956 Chevy found on the used car market or in a junk yard. It might cost many thousands of dollars to obtain a replacement vehicle and restore it to the same condition prior to a loss. So, you'd want to insure it for an amount you could determine.

But this coverage is expensive. The cherry 1956 Chevy that you declare worth $50,000 may cost more to insure than a new Mercedes that costs the same amount. And the insurance company has to agree to your determined amount.

> **Sports and luxury cars are more difficult to insure. Many people find out, once they've bought their first high-performance sports car, that the insurance can cost as much as monthly payments on the car. Even when the cost isn't that drastic, it will be significant.**

If you want to indulge a taste for exotic or high-performance cars, factor in between 50 and 100 percent of the annual cost of buying and keeping the cars for insurance. Among other things, if the value of your car is higher than the state-required liability minimum, you'll have to buy supplemental or additional underinsured motorists coverage.

Even if you're not driving a Ferarri or Lambourghini, a sports car can cost a lot to insure. Most insurance companies classify car models in one of four groups—**standard, high performance, sports** and **high performance sports**. The last three classifications all include higher premiums.

> Whether your car is a sedan or a sports coupe, installing safety features will help control insurance costs. Most insurance companies offer discounts for cars that have air bags, anti-lock brakes, automatic seat belts and anti-theft alarm systems.

SINGLE VERSUS MULTIPLE CAR POLICIES

Insurance policies are often divided into two categories—one for single car risks, and one for multi-car risks. Multi-car factors are lower than single car factors, because they include a discount for insuring two or more cars. This means insuring a second car will be much less expensive than insuring two cars separately.

> Multi-car risks often include multiple drivers as well. Especially when young drivers are in the group, this is what drives up costs.

There are several reasons young drivers are expensive. Auto accidents were the most frequent cause of death among people 6 to 33 years old in 1992. In 1993, more than **5,400 teenagers died** on American roads, and half of the deaths were **alcohol-related**.

THE POLICY'S DECLARATIONS PAGE

The place where you can express all of your individual insurance needs is the **Declarations Page** of your auto insurance policy. We'll briefly consider the various parts of the standard Declarations Page issued by the Insurance Services Office.

You may hear the Declarations Page referred to as a Declarations Sheet, Dec Sheet, or Dec Page.

CHAPTER 2

DECLARATIONS

(Policy Number) _____

(Previous Policy Number) _____ **(COMPANY NAME)** _____

Policy Period   12:01 a.m. Standard Time   From: To: (Years)

Named Insured and mailing address

(Number, Street, Apartment, Town or City, County, State, Zip Code)

Description of Auto(s) or Trailer(s)

Auto	Year	Trade Name - Model	VIN	Sym	Age
1					
2					
3					

The Auto(s) or Trailer(s) described in this policy is principally garaged at the above address unless otherwise stated.

(Number, Street, Apartment, Town or City, County, State, Zip Code)

HOW TO FIGURE OUT HOW MUCH CAR INSURANCE YOU NEED

Coverage is provided where a premium and a limit of liability is shown for the coverage

Coverages	Limit of Liability		Premium		
			Auto 1	Auto 2	Auto 3
A. Liability	$_____	each accident	$_____	$_____	$_____
B. Medical Payments	$_____	each person	$_____	$_____	$_____
C. Uninsured Motorists	$_____	each accident	$_____	$_____	$_____
D. Damage to Auto					
1. Collision Loss	ACV minus $_____	Deductible	$_____	$_____	$_____
2. Other Than Collision Loss	ACV minus $_____	Deductible	$_____	$_____	$_____
(Towing and Labor Costs)	($_____	each disablement)	$_____	$_____	$_____
	(ACV means Actual Cash Value)		($_____	$_____	$_____)

Endorsements made part of this Policy at time of issue:

Endorsement Premium $_____

Total Premium $_____

Loss Payee:

(Name and address)

(This policy shall not be valid unless countersigned by our authorized agent)

(Countersignature Date)   (Agency at:)

_____ Agent)

(_____

(Company Officer)

Title

38

All completed Declarations Pages will contain the **policy number**, and this item of information is extremely important since virtually all insurance companies file their policies by policy number rather than by the insured's name. The space for "Previous Policy Number" may be left blank if the insured's last policy was not written with this particular insurance company. Some companies will type "New" in the space rather than leaving it blank.

Section 1 of the Declarations Page also contains the name of the **insurance company**, and you may see more than one company name printed here if a number of insurance companies are part of the same organization or group.

Sections 3 and 5 of the Declarations Page are related, so we will discuss them together before we discuss Section 4. Section 3 identifies the **named insured** by **name and mailing address**. Many other people can be covered by an insurance policy besides the one whose name appears in the Declarations. Although other people may be covered under some circumstances, the policy is still an agreement between the named insured and the insurance company. In some cases, a married couple may choose to include both spouses as named insureds—otherwise the named insured is usually just one person.

Section 5 indicates the address at which the insured vehicles are **principally garaged** (that is, most often kept), if it is different from the named insured's mailing address. Such a difference might occur if the named insured uses a post office box as a mailing address, or lives in one city but keeps a car at a vacation home located in a different city or state. The insurance company will use the garaging address when determining what premium you'll pay.

While there may appear to be no relationship between the policy period and the named insured's address, there is a very important connection. The effective and expiration dates of the policy are as of 12:01 a.m. Standard Time in the county in which the vehicle is principally garaged. The only time this becomes important is when an accident occurs close to midnight on the day the policy becomes effective or expires.

Section 4 of the Declarations Page describes the covered autos or trailers being insured by the policy. **Model year** in this line means the manufacturer's model year. As you may know, auto manufacturers usually start selling their new models in the fall of the previous year—for example, 1994 models would be introduced in the fall of 1993. It is the model year and not the year of purchase that appears in the Declarations.

Related to model year is the **age** of a vehicle, which is derived from the model year and is shown in the last part of Section 4. According to the age group rule, the model year changes each October 1, regardless of when manufacturers actually introduce new models. For example, after October 1, 1994, all 1995 models would be classified as age group one, 1994 autos would be age group two, and 1993 vehicles would be age group three. The maximum age is six, so all vehicles more than five years old are classified as age group six.

Trade name and **model** are also manufacturer information, as is VIN (the **Vehicle Identification Number** assigned to an individual car by the manufacturer). **Symbol** is a number assigned by the insurance company to represent the cost of the car when new. Both the symbol and model year (or age) of covered autos will be used by the insurance company in determining the policy premium.

The first part of Section 6 lists coverages which are available under a Personal Auto Policy.

For both **collision loss** and **other than collision loss**, Section 6 in the Declarations, the limits of liability are specified as "ACV minus $_____ Deductible" are used.

Section 7 of the Declarations is where the insurance company lists the form numbers of **endorsements** to the particular policy when it is issued.

A **Change Endorsement** is issued when endorsements are attached after the effective date, and whatever endorsements are to be attached to the policy will be listed on the Change Endorsement rather than in the Declarations.

When endorsements add coverage to a policy, there is almost always an **additional premium** charged. Section 6 of the Declarations includes a line for towing and labor cost coverage, even though an endorsement must be attached. Premiums charged for endorsements are added together and shown in Section 7.

The final line in Section 7 of the Declarations includes space for entering the **total policy premium**. This is the total amount the insured will pay for all coverages for which limits and premiums are shown and for any additional endorsements which are attached.

The last part of the Declarations Page, Section 9, includes spaces for a date and signatures. Notice the statement: "This policy shall not be valid unless countersigned by our authorized agent." The signature of an insurance company officer is frequently preprinted on the blank forms. But an agent must sign the completed Declarations to make the policy valid, and the date of countersignature and the city and state in which the agent's office is located must be entered as well. Some agents will also type or rubber stamp the agency name and address on the Declarations, but this is not necessary.

A final caveat: To extend your liability, medical payments, uninsured motorists, collision and other than collision coverage to motor homes, motorcycles, golf carts, etc., you must endorse your auto policy with a **Miscellaneous Type Vehicle Endorsement**[1].

CHOOSING COVERAGE AND PREMIUMS

We'll consider the best ways to shop for cost-effective insurance in Chapter 9. But, to some degree, figuring out what kind of insurance you need requires you to make the kind of choices that control how much you'll spend on auto coverage.

If you are driving an older car with a **low replacement value**, you might want to drop your collision coverage in order to reduce your premium. However, if you cause an accident causing damage to your car, you would not be reimbursed at all for the vehicle, so you should only do this if you are willing to pay the **entire cost** of repairing or replacing that vehicle. An-

---
[1] For more on these and other kinds of endorsements, see Chapter 8.

other factor that affects the final premium charged is the size of the **deductibles** you select to apply to collision and comprehensive damages.

> Many different elements make up the premium. You can pick and choose coverages and in some cases manipulate the menu to get more protection for less money.

Resist the temptation to minimize liability coverage. The risk of injuring or killing another person is the **largest risk** you face when driving. You should consider carrying limits that are higher than those required by law, especially if you have a home or other assets to protect.

> If you cause an accident and are found to be liable, after the insurance company has paid the limits of the policy, you will have to pay any remaining damages out of your own pocket. The more you own, the more liability insurance you need.

In some situations, you should also consider carrying increased limits for **uninsured/underinsured motorists** coverage. In the event you are in an accident with an uninsured driver or a driver whose coverage is insufficient to pay the damages they are responsible for, your insurance company will step in and pay your additional costs.

Medical payments coverage is optional in some states, and if you do most of your driving alone and have good health insurance coverage you might decide not to buy it and avoid paying twice for similar coverage. However, if you often have people other than family members in your car, you should keep your medical payments coverage because in the event of an accident, injuries to all passengers would be covered.

> Passengers who are family members could collect under your health insurance policy, but nonfamily members would have to sue you for negligence to collect under your automobile liability insurance.

Some states allow **benefit stacking** as an optional coverage. This coverage means that you can add the uninsured motorists limits from insurance on several different cars to apply to a single claim. But be careful about stacking—you obviously shouldn't buy it if you only have one car. (Some states have been accused of allowing stacking charges to be applied to all insurance policies.)

The standard policy form excludes liability coverage for any auto which you either own or regularly available for your use—but is not one of your "covered autos."

The purpose of this exclusion is simply to make sure that all "covered autos" are declared on the policy, and that a premium is charged for them. Although the policy will cover your occasional use of non-owned autos, it will not provide free insurance for autos which you own or use regularly if they are not shown on the policy.

> For example, a car furnished by your employer for business and incidental personal use is not covered.

Another exclusion removes coverage for any cars owned by or furnished for the regular use of any family member if they are not "covered autos." But this exclusion does not apply to you as the named insured (which means that the policy does provide coverage for you when you're using a non-covered auto which belongs to a family member).

> An example: Your spouse uses an auto furnished by your spouse's employer. There would be no medical payments for accidents occurring while you or your spouse use the auto furnished by the employer, since the presumption is that coverage would be furnished by the employer's commercial auto policy.

CONCLUSION

This chapter has given you a framework for calculating your auto insurance needs. But before you make any decision about the insurance you buy, you should have a working knowledge of the mechanics of car insurance. The next section of this book, which includes chapters 3 through 8, deals with these mechanics in detail.

CHAPTER 3

HOW CAR INSURANCE WORKS

To make informed decisions about what kind of auto insurance you need, how much to buy and how to make a claim, you need to understand the basic mechanics of how the coverage works.

In this chapter, we will consider some of the basic terms controlling how car insurance works. In the chapters that follow, we'll consider some of the specific mechanics in greater detail.

CONTRACTUAL TERMS

An insurance policy is a written agreement between two **parties**. One party is **the insured person**, and the other party is **the insurance company**.

An insurance policy is also a **legally binding contract**. As is true with all contracts, an insurance policy describes the rights and obligations of each party. In addition, the policy identifies how much the policyholder must pay to receive those rights—this amount is called the "premium." The policy also identifies how much the insurance company is obligated to pay if certain events occur—these amounts are **limits of insurance** or **limits of liability**.

As we've seen already, a lot of the specific information relating to an insurance policy appears on the **Declarations Page**. This page includes all the things which are particular to a given policyholder—the names of the **people covered** by the policy, the **dates** it's in effect and the **cars covered**.

> When you purchase a Personal Auto Policy, only those accidents that occur during the policy period shown on the Declarations Page are covered. The policy period is therefore very important in determining whether coverage applies.

The beginning date of an insurance policy is called the **effective date**, since it is the date on which coverage begins to be effective. When coverage under a policy stops, we say that the policy has expired, and thus the date on which coverage stops or ends is called the **expiration date**.

There is also a reference to a time of day with respect to the effective date and expiration date. It is important to pinpoint the time as well as the date on which coverage begins and ends.

> The Declarations Page will either mention or refer to any specific kinds of coverage added or dropped from the standard policy.

CHAPTER 3

ELIGIBILITY

Particular people, vehicles, and situations are eligible for coverage under a Personal Auto Policy. The conditions of eligibility are sprinkled throughout the policy and the manual rules that govern how and when a policy may be written. We will consolidate most of them here.

To be eligible, a vehicle must be owned by one of the following:

- an **individual**;
- a **husband and wife** who are residents of the same household;
- two or more **relatives** other than husband and wife, or two or more unrelated people in the same household, but only if a Joint Ownership Coverage Endorsement is attached to the policy;
- a **farm family co-partnership** or farm family corporation.

Only **private passenger vehicles** are eligible for coverage under the Personal Auto Policy. To be considered a private passenger auto, the vehicle must, first of all, be a four-wheel motor vehicle.

Sedans and station wagons qualify as "private passenger autos" for coverage under a Personal Auto Policy. But pickup trucks, panel trucks, and vans may also be considered "private passenger autos" and be eligible for coverage if they satisfy the following requirements:

- be owned by insured persons,
- have a Gross Vehicle Weight of less than 10,000 pounds,
- not be used in a freight or delivery business.

But sedans and station wagons do not qualify as private passenger autos if they are being used in a taxi or limousine service.

> In other words, sedans and station wagons may be used in a freight or delivery business if they are only transporting cargo (products, materials or packages) for a fee.

A leased auto is usually treated as if it were owned and may be covered under a Personal Auto Policy. An important distinction here: Renting is not the same as leasing. (We considered how insurance applies to rented cars in Chapter 1.)

Most policies deal with individuals or husband and wife as **named insureds**. However, you should be aware that under a different ownership situation, such as when unrelated people jointly own an auto or when coverage is added for an employee of a named insured, insurance companies use the more expensive rates for **all others** or **additional persons** instead of the individual or husband and wife rate.

CHAPTER 3

MEDICAL PAYMENTS

One important aspect of auto insurance is **medical payments coverage**. This coverage pays reasonable medical expenses incurred by you, members of your family, and passengers for bodily injuries sustained while riding in your car.

Coverage also applies to you and your family members while riding in another automobile or if injured as pedestrians by an automobile. The medical payments coverage allows immediate payment to you or other covered persons regardless of fault.

> Medical payments coverage is sometimes called a "no-fault" coverage, because it is paid without regard to fault or negligence. It is not necessary to determine who was at fault in order for coverage to apply.

Immediacy isn't the only consideration in medical claims. Injuries resulting from an accident can sometimes require treatment over a long period of time. Sometimes one treatment is rendered immediately (like the setting of a broken bone) and another treatment is required later (like surgery to put a pin in the bone that was broken). There may be a long delay between the first treatment and the final treatment for an injury.

For this reason, the Insuring Agreement section in many standard auto policies include a **time limita-**

tion on expenses covered by the medical payments insurance.

Medical payments apply **per person**. Payments made under the medical payments provision are offset against any payments made to an injured person under liability (Part A) or uninsured motorists (Part C) coverage.

Assume that an injured person has $3,000 in medical expenses and is later awarded $10,000 under the uninsured motorists coverage because the other party did not carry liability coverage. The injured person would receive the difference between $10,000 and the $3,000 previously paid, or a net of $7,000.

Either Liability[1] or Medical Payments coverage—or both—might apply to injuries to a **passenger in your car**. Liability coverage would depend, of course, on whether you were legally responsible for the passenger's injuries. Medical Payments coverage would apply regardless of legal liability, subject to certain conditions.

STACKING CLAIMS

A big issue in auto insurance medical claims is a practice known as **stacking**. This means combining medical liability limits from several insured vehicles—or even several different policies—to cover one big claim.

Stacking insurance against a single claim allows drivers who insure more than one vehicle with the same insurance company to combine specific kinds of coverage from all insured vehicles.

---

[1] For more on Liability coverage, see Chapter 5.

CHAPTER 3

> For example, if you have $50,000 of uninsured/underinsured motorists coverage on each of two cars, you could stack them and apply $100,000 of coverage toward one accident.

In December 1994, the New Jersey supreme court ruled that an **anti-stacking provision** in the state's no-fault auto insurance system didn't prevent a man who suffered catastrophic injuries in a motorcycle accident from recovering personal injury protection (PIP) benefits from two insurance companies.

The 7-0 ruling resolved the case of Brian Lihou, who was seriously hurt in 1987 when the motorcycle he was riding collided with a car. Because he was riding a motorcycle, his medical bills were not covered under the basic PIP benefits coverage of his auto insurance policy with the state-run Joint Underwriting Association.

The policy, however, contained an extended medical expense benefits provision, which furnished up to $10,000 coverage for injuries in motorcycle accidents. So the JUA paid Lihou the $10,000.

Lihou, who was living with his mother at the time, also sought coverage under her auto insurance with Aetna Casualty, on which he was listed as a driver. Aetna refused to pay, arguing the anti-stacking provision prohibited Lihou from being paid by two insurance companies. Lihou sued.

A trial court agreed with Aetna, as did the appeals court. But the state supreme court ordered Aetna to pay. In a nine-page, unsigned opinion, the justices concluded:

> Supporting our determination are sound public-policy considerations, perhaps best illustrated by the circumstances of this case. [Lihou]'s medical expenses exceed $35,000.
>
> Requiring Aetna to pay its $10,000 limit—the maximum that the carrier can provide under the [insurance] commissioner's regulation—will result in no windfall to [Lihou], no double recovery of any medical expense, and indeed [Lihou] will be left with a balance of over $15,000 in uncompensated expenses.

To stack insurance coverages after an auto accident, you need **more than one** insured vehicle. But insurance companies will sometimes charge policyholders with a single car for stacking privileges.

> If you own one car, there's nothing to stack and no reason to pay for the right to do so.

In the fall of 1995, a group of Pennsylvania policyholders filed a series of class-action suits charging the state and all auto insurance companies doing business there with systematically charging drivers with one car for **non-existent stacking rights.**

"You're paying [stacking premiums], even though it can be of no benefit to you," said attorney Joseph Roda, who helped draft the suits. "It's a **windfall for the insurance companies**, because nobody can ever file a claim for it."

Roda said single-vehicle drivers had been charged for stacking since 1990, when a Pennsylvania auto insurance reform law known as Act 6 took effect. The law allowed **all drivers to reject stacking rights** and reduce their overall insurance bill. But, unless single-vehicle drivers signed a waiver, they could be charged an extra premium—one which **wasn't itemized on most bills.**

DAMAGE TO YOUR CAR

You might hear people refer to "physical damage coverage" when they talk about car insurance. That term was used until **Damage to Your Auto** was introduced with the standard ISO Personal Auto Policy. The two terms have the same meaning. Coverage for damage to your auto is divided into two categories.

Collision coverage refers to direct or accidental physical damage to your car as the result of upset (turning over) or impact with another vehicle or object (other than a bird or animal).

The second loss category for damage to your car is called, not surprisingly, **other than collision** loss. Historically, this has been known as **comprehensive** coverage. This is a broad category that includes many types of loss.

> Collision pays for traffic accident damages, and comprehensive pays for other types of damage such as hail or a tree falling on your car. Collision coverage typically accounts for about 30 percent of the annual cost of an auto insurance policy and comprehensive accounts for about 15 percent.

Based on the names of the coverages, it might appear that when you purchase both "collision" and "other than collision" coverage that any possible loss situation would be covered. This is not quite true, since there are a few **exclusions** in the policy as you will see later. But purchasing both coverages does give you extremely broad coverage for direct and accidental loss to insured vehicles.

ASSIGNED RISK

In most states, if no insurance company will sell you car insurance you can buy coverage from a **state-run company** or an **assigned risk plan**. Insurance policies written by these alternative markets tend to be expensive and offer more limited coverage than standard policies.

A state-run insurance company is simply that. An assigned risk plan is a co-operative enterprise that all insurance companies doing business in the state must join. The plan constructs a policy (again, usually expensive and limited) that it will sell to people whose driving records or location **disqualify them from standard coverage**. It then forces the participating insurance companies to take a number of assigned-risk policies.

Insurance companies usually have to take a number of assigned-risk drivers **proportional to their marketshare** in the state. Big companies have to take more, small companies fewer.

> State-run companies and assigned risk plans both serve the same purpose, have similar structures and share common problems. Both also share fairly frequent financial problems. In most cases, you do best to avoid them if you can.

In New York, drivers in the mainstream market (sometimes called the **voluntary** or **commercial** market) subsidize the assigned risk pool. Insurance companies fear that the premiums they collect from drivers in the assigned risk pool won't offset the claims they'll have to pay off because of rising coverage minimums.

Michigan drivers are forced to **subsidize** insurance sold through the Michigan Automobile Insurance Placement Facility (MAIPF) to drivers unable to obtain insurance in the private market because they're high risks. MAIPF writes this insurance at a loss (averaging about 1 or 2 percent of total premiums), which is then passed on to private insurance companies which then charge it to customers as a **cost of doing business**.

A more troubled example: In early 1995, R. Terry Haskins, chief operating officer of New Jersey's Market Transition Facility (MTF), and Marshall Selikoff, trustee of the state's Joint Underwriting Association (JUA), resigned.

The MTF was a state-run insurance company. The JUA was an assigned risk plan. Most states don't have both forms—but New Jersey had had so many problems for so long that it needed all the alternatives markets it could find.

A few weeks before Haskins and Selikoff resigned, former Deputy Insurance Commissioner Jasper Jackson had charged that the deficit-ridden insurance pools were poorly run and said former Insurance Commissioner Samuel Fortunato recommended in 1993 that both men be fired.

Companies administering claims for the MTF were paying accident settlements without attempting to negotiate lower awards with plaintiffs' insurance companies.

The JUA had been founded in 1984 to cover motorists who were unable to obtain auto insurance in the private market. At the time, insurance companies said they could not make money in densely populated New Jersey and refused to write policies for many residents. The JUA grew to insure 2 million policyholders and ran up a debt of $3.6 billion.

In 1990, Governor Jim Florio abolished the JUA and mandated that auto insurance companies write policies for all motorists with eight or fewer motor vehicle points. To ease the transition of drivers into the private market, Florio created the MTF to serve as a temporary pool to insure drivers. Like the JUA, the MTF developed a debt, which officials said reached $1.3 billion in 1994.

The last JUA policy had expired in 1990, and the last MTF policy had expired in 1993. But the pools were still paying claims filed by accident victims. In 1994, state officials had to stop paying claims for MTF accident victims because the reserves in the pool had dropped below $50 million.

> In general, it's best to stay away from assigned risk insurance. If you have no choice, call the state agency that runs the program—or a local insurance agent—and find out why you have to use the plan. Ask the state agency what you can do to improve your application. Get out of the assigned risk plan as soon as you can.

HOW THE INSURANCE COMPANY PAYS

The insurance company will usually only pay the **actual cash value** or the cost to repair or replace the damaged or stolen property, whichever is less. However, coverage for a non-owned trailer is limited to $500. In all settlements, depreciation and the condition of the vehicle are considered in determining the ACV at the time of loss.

The following section of ISO's standard auto policy describes the various options that are open to the insurance company in settling a loss which is covered by the policy:

> We may pay for loss in money or repair or replace the damaged or stolen property. We may, at our expense, return any stolen property to:
>
> 1. You; or
>
> 2. The address shown in this policy.
>
> If we return stolen property we will pay for any damage resulting from the theft. We may keep all or part of the property at an agreed or appraised value.
>
> If we pay for loss in money, our payment will include the applicable sales tax for the damaged or stolen property.

Indemnification for the loss may be **payment in money or replacement of the property**. Stolen property may be returned to you and payment made for any damage, or the company may keep the property and pay you an agreed or appraised amount in money.

If you think you're owed more than your insurance company has offered you in cash or for repairs, you can challenge the offer. The standard policy also outlines this process:

> If we and you do not agree on the amount of loss, either may demand an appraisal of the loss. In this event, each party will select a competent appraiser. The two appraisers will se-

lect an umpire. The appraisers will state separately the actual cash value and the amount of loss. If they fail to agree, they will submit their differences to the umpire. A decision agreed to by any two will be binding. Each party will:

1. Pay its chosen appraiser; and

2. Bear the expenses of the appraisal and umpire equally.

We do not waive any of our rights under this policy by agreeing to an appraisal.

This provision is similar to the **arbitration provision** that some states require in insurance disputes. The arbitration condition usually applies in cases where the insured and insurance company cannot agree either on whether a loss is covered or on the amount of damages.

The physical damage appraisal condition applies only when the insured and insurance company cannot agree on the amount of a covered loss.

GENERAL PROVISIONS

The standard auto insurance policy is also defined by a number of **general provisions** which limit and qualify coverage. Among the most important of these:

- what happens if you declare bankruptcy,
- how you or the company can change the policy,
- how the policy period and territory limit coverage, and

- how different policies that apply to the same accident relate to each other.

We'll consider each of these issues in turn.

BANKRUPTCY

> Bankruptcy or insolvency of the "insured" shall not relieve us of any obligations under this policy.

The wording of some indemnification contracts would relieve the insurance company of its payment responsibility if you become bankrupt or insolvent. This clause makes it definite as to the responsibility of the insurance company to pay under these circumstances.

CHANGES

> This policy contains all the agreements between you and us. Its terms may not be changed or waived except by endorsement issued by us.
>
> If there is a change to the information used to develop the policy premium, we may adjust your premium....
>
> If we make a change which broadens coverage under this edition of your policy without additional premium charge, that change will automatically apply to your policy as of the date we implement the change in your state....

Both you and your insurance company may want to make a change to a part of the policy, and this section describes the conditions for making any such change.

The policy is the entire agreement between you and the company, and its provisions can only be changed or waived by an endorsement issued by the company. Any premium adjustments are made as of the date of the change.

> If during the policy term the coverage should be broadened, the broader terms will automatically apply to the policy as long as there is no additional premium required for the broadened coverage. However, if a change involves both broader and more restrictive provisions, the changed provisions shall not apply to the policy until it is renewed.

POLICY PERIOD AND TERRITORY

This policy applies only to accidents and losses which occur:

1. During the policy period as shown in the Declarations; and

2. Within the policy territory.

The policy territory is:

1. The United States of America, its territories or possessions;

2. Puerto Rico; or

3. Canada.

This policy also applies to loss to, or accidents involving, "your covered auto" while being transported between their ports.

This provision states that coverage applies only to accidents or losses that occur during the policy period and within the policy territory. It also defines the policy territory.

The policy only applies to losses which occur during the policy period in the described territory. It is interesting to note that an auto being transported from New York to Hawaii via the Panama Canal would be covered under the policy.

TWO OR MORE AUTO POLICIES

> If this policy and any other auto insurance policy issued to you by us apply to the same accident, the maximum limit of our liability under all the policies shall not exceed the highest applicable limit of liability under any one policy.

This provision specifies the maximum amount that the insurance company will pay if you have coverage under **two or more policies issued by the same company** and have an accident for which both apply. (This differs from the "Other Insurance" clauses that appear in a standard policy—those provisions relate to other policies issued by other insurance companies.)

When an accident occurs, an injured person may be entitled to recover under **more than one coverage.** When an accident is covered by more than one insurance policy, often one policy is considered **primary coverage,** meaning that that policy would pay first up to its policy limit. Then, if the claim was greater than the primary policy's limit, the second policy involved would pay the excess amount of the claim, up to its limit of liability. The second policy is then said to be **excess coverage**.

If two or more policies issued by the same company apply to an accident, the highest limit of liability on one policy applies, not the total limits of all policies. This is intended to prevent stacking.

SUBROGATION

The standard auto policy also includes a provision known as a **subrogation clause**. This provision says that if the insurance company has made a payment under the policy to or for any person, and if that person has a legal right to recover for that loss from another person, then the insurance company is subrogated to that right, and may seek recovery from the responsible third party.

Specifically, this provision says:

> If we make a payment under this policy and the person to or for whom payment was made has a right to recover damages from another we shall be subrogated to that right. That person shall do:
>
> 1. Whatever is necessary to enable us to exercise our rights; and
>
> 2. Nothing after loss to prejudice them.
>
> However, our rights in this paragraph do not apply...against any person using "your covered auto" with a reasonable belief that that person is entitled to do so.

> If we make a payment under this policy and the person to or for whom payment is made recovers damages from another, that person shall:
>
> 1. Hold in trust for us the proceeds of the recovery; and
>
> 2. Reimburse us to the extent of our payment.

If the company makes a payment to you for injury or damage caused by another person, the company takes over your rights to recover the payments from the party causing the injury or damage. You must cooperate with the company to assist in recovery (such as appearing in court as a witness) and may do nothing to impair the rights of the company (such as signing a settlement agreement with the other party).

This provision also describes the insurance company's right to be reimbursed if any person to or for whom payment has been made under the insurance policy does, in fact, later recover any damages from the person who is responsible.

For physical damage coverage, the insurance company does not have subrogation rights against anyone using a "covered auto" with permission, because that would undermine the intent of the coverage. It may only seek recovery from other parties who may be liable (and who should have their own insurance policy).

If the party to or for whom the company has made payment for damages or injury should receive any reimbursement from the other party, that person is required to hold the money in trust and reimburse the company for any amounts that it has paid.

CONCLUSION

In this chapter, we've taken a brief look at some technical aspects of car insurance. In the next four chapters, we'll focus on particular mechanical aspects of how this insurance works.

HOW CAR INSURANCE WORKS

CHAPTER 4

IMPORTANT DEFINITIONS

Every specialized field has its own language—and auto insurance is no exception. Because insurance policies are legal contracts, the language in them has a big effect on how they work.

The language of an insurance policy is as important to understand as the mechanics of the policy.

In this chapter, we'll focus on the practical issues that policy language and definitions raise.

To get started, here's a quick list of some important definitions:

- *Loss* as used in an insurance policy does not generally mean *misplacement*—*loss* means a **direct financial loss** of value as a result of situations which are covered by the policy.

- The phrase *your covered auto* is used throughout the policy to refer to the specific car or cars listed in the Declarations Page. A car has to be listed—usually by

IMPORTANT DEFINITIONS

  vehicle identification number—in order to be considered a covered auto. It means any autos listed in the Declarations section, other vehicles acquired during the policy period and temporary substitute autos or trailers.

- The phrase *non-owned autos* is a relatively recent addition to standard policy forms written by some insurance companies. It relates to coverage for cars you've **borrowed or rented**.

- For a contract to be binding each party to the contract must give what is known as *consideration*. Your consideration is paying the premium and abiding by the policy conditions, while the company's consideration is the protection of you and payment of claims as provided by the policy.

- A *collision* does not have to involve smashing into something—damage caused by the **upset or overturn** of a covered auto is collision damage. Nor does it have to involve smashing into another vehicle—**hitting an object** (such as a tree, bridge or mailbox) is a collision.

A caveat: Colliding with animals or birds is not considered collision according to standard policies, and the damage would be covered only if **other than collision** (OTC) coverage has been purchased.

These quick definitions involve basic, focused concepts that are relatively easy to understand. Other concepts are more difficult. Those are the cases in which definitions become crucial issues.

INTERPRETATION

The most difficult cause of coverage disputes is **vague or subjective language** in the insurance policy.

> For example, in the section of the standard policy that deals with the duties you have after an accident, you're told that you have to inform the insurance company promptly.

The use of subjective words like *promptly* lead to problems of **interpretation** in some cases. In the **duties section**, its use is intended to provide the flexibility necessary for a policyholder in reporting some cases.

> You might be hospitalized and be in serious condition for several days or weeks after an accident. Family members might be unaware of the insurance policy requirements. Such inability to report immediately after an accident would be taken into consideration by the insurance company in reviewing your claim. It's not likely that coverage would be denied because of this kind of delay.

IMPORTANT DEFINITIONS

Insurance companies tend to shy away from subjective or interpretive language, though. As we've seen elsewhere, ambiguous language creates a **presumption of coverage**. As one court ruled:

> To find coverage does not rewrite the contract; it merely broadly interprets ambiguous terms against the insurer so as to effectuate the policy behind the law to provide comprehensive insurance coverage to innocent parties injured by uninsured vehicles.

Cars and other motor vehicles should be titled in the name of only one person—the named insured on the auto policy.

An example: Under Florida law, both the operator and the owner of a vehicle involved in an accident may be sued. If the vehicle is owned by the driver, assets owned by the driver's spouse or owned by them both as tenants by the entireties are still protected.

To avoid liability disputes, most attorneys and smart insurance agents recommend that once children turn 18 they should be **the legal owners** of the cars they drive. The move doesn't help with younger children because parents still might be found liable in an accident for failing to supervise the actions of a minor.

CHAPTER 4

THE DEFINITIONS SECTION

In an effort to combat vague or subjective language, the standard auto insurance policy gives special attention to definitions. After the **Declarations Page**, the next place where basic information is determined is the definitions section.

The definitions section generally describes:

1) who is covered,
2) when and where coverage applies, and
3) what vehicles are covered.

The biggest part of the definitions section focuses on the **who** and **what** issues that impact coverage. To illustrate, we'll consider some of the definitions that appear in the standard auto policy.

> A. Throughout this policy, "you" and "your" refer to:
>
> 1. The "named insured" shown in the Declarations; and
>
> 2. The spouse if a resident of the same household.

Insurance policies used to be much more formal and included numerous references to the named insured and the company (meaning the insurer issuing the contract). In recent years policies were rewritten to make them easier to read. For this reason, you'll find references to *you* and *we* instead of more formal references to *the insured* and *insurer*.

IMPORTANT DEFINITIONS

The person or persons named on the policy are called **named insureds**; however, if only one name is shown, the **spouse** of that person is also considered to be a named insured if a resident of the same household.

Other persons who reside in the same **household** and are related to a named insured by blood, marriage, or adoption, or are wards or foster children, are called *family members*, and are also covered when the policy refers to *insured persons or you*.

Although the policy definition does not say so, a **family member** includes a student temporarily living away at school (private school, college or university).

Definitions of *household* are always difficult in insurance coverage disputes. But they get particularly convoluted in auto coverage cases.

> B. "We," "us" and "our" refer to the Company providing this insurance.
>
> C. For purposes of this policy, a private passenger type auto shall be deemed to be owned by a person if leased:
>
> 1. Under a written agreement to that person; and
>
> 2. For a continuous period of at least 6 months.
>
> Other words and phrases are defined. They are in quotation marks when used.
>
> D. "Bodily injury" means bodily harm, sickness or disease, including death that results.
>
> E. "Business" includes trade, profession or occupation.

F. "Family member" means a person related to you by blood, marriage or adoption who is a resident of your household. This includes a ward or foster child.

G. "Occupying" means in, upon, getting in, on, out or off.

H. "Property damage" means physical injury to, destruction of or loss of use of tangible property.

To prevent any **misinterpretation** of the coverage provided by this policy, the terms *bodily injury, business* and *property damage* are specifically defined.

The term *occupying* is defined so broadly that it includes most situations involving any injury as a result of the **use or maintenance** of an automobile. It means, in addition to riding in an automobile, entering or alighting from, or getting on or off a vehicle. This includes such things as jumping from the bed of a pickup truck and injuring an ankle or slipping off a curb while getting into an automobile.

The term *occupying* is used throughout the policy in reference to a person's location in relationship to a vehicle. A person who is occupying a covered auto is not necessarily inside the vehicle.

Specific provisions apply to pickups or vans only. They must have a gross weight of under 10,000 pounds, not be used in a freight or delivery business (delivery of goods, parcels or materials for a fee), and must not be insured under any other insurance policy. The incidental delivery of goods if your business is farming, ranching, installations, service or repair is permitted.

IMPORTANT DEFINITIONS

LOCATION AND CONTENTS

There is sometimes lack of clarity and disagreement between insurance companies and policyholders as to exactly where a **vehicle is located**.

One factor that might enter into the determination could be whether the policyholder has a **permanent residence**, such as a house or apartment—if not, the person might be living out of the vehicle. The standard policy doesn't cover vehicles being used as residences.

> The percentage of time spent "living out of" the auto could also be a factor—a two-week vacation in a camper would probably not be considered "use of a vehicle as a residence."

Also, if the auto is **parked at one site and never moved**, it would more likely be considered to be used as a premises.

However, in any of these cases, coverage would always apply while the auto is being used for **transportation** purposes.

Contents of a vehicle or personal effects are not covered under a standard Personal Auto Policy. This may seem unfair, because all drivers carry belongings around in their cars. But, in order to make the **risk projections** for auto insurance feasible, insurance companies can't calculate such a changing factor.

When you buy insurance on a car, the premiums that the insurance company charges for **physical damage** coverage ("collision" and "other than collision") are based on the **maximum amount** that the insurance company might have to pay if the vehicle were a total loss.

> For example, the insurance company might charge $200 for one year's coverage on an $8,000 car. The most the company could expect to pay to repair or replace the car would be $8,000. But it has no control over the value of any items you might carry in the vehicle on any given day. If you were transporting a $100,000 painting in an $8,000 car and the car and painting were destroyed in a collision, the insurance company would be unfairly penalized if it had to pay out $108,000 when it had collected premium for only $8,000 of value.

Personal property items (such as clothing, cameras, sporting equipment, tools and all the things you carry around in your car) should be insured under a different type of policy. Most people have this coverage under a **homeowners** insurance policy, but coverage is also available under **Personal Property Floaters** and other specialized property insurance policy forms.

WHO'S COVERED

As you might guess, the biggest dispute next to how an insurance policy works is who's covered. This is

IMPORTANT DEFINITIONS

another issue controlled by the definitions established in the policy itself. So, let's consider what the standard policy form says.

> "Insured" as used in this Part means:
>
> 1. You or any "family member" for the ownership, maintenance or use of any auto or "trailer."
>
> 2. Any person using "your covered auto."
>
> 3. For "your covered auto," any person or organization but only with respect to legal responsibility for acts or omissions of a person for whom coverage is afforded under this Part.
>
> 4. For any auto or "trailer," other than "your covered auto," any other person or organization but only with respect to legal responsibility for acts or omissions of you or any "family member" for whom coverage is afforded under this Part. This provision applies only if the person or organization does not own or hire the auto or "trailer."

The named insured and family members are insured with respect to *any auto*.

An example: You are covered under your policy when you borrow a friend's car. Any other person using "your covered auto" is also covered under your policy—your friend would be covered while using your car.

CHAPTER 4

In certain situations, other persons or organizations may be insured with respect to their legal liability for the acts of an insured person.

> If you use your covered auto while doing volunteer work for a church, youth group, or charitable organization and are involved in an accident, the organization would be protected by your policy if it were held liable for your acts.

For autos you do not own, another person or organization would be protected under your policy only if they did not own the vehicle.

> If you borrow your neighbor's station wagon to transport Red Cross workers to a meeting hall where they will solicit blood donors, the Red Cross would be protected; but if you were driving a station wagon owned by the Red Cross, it would not be an "insured" under your policy. You would still be insured as the driver, but the Red Cross should carry primary liability coverage for its own exposure.

If a person is using an insured auto and is not a **named insured** or a **family member**, that person must have a reasonable belief of being entitled to do so. Usually this would involve **permission by the owner.**

IMPORTANT DEFINITIONS

Reasonable expectation is an important issue in coverage disputes. If a person is operating the auto contrary to specific instructions not to do so, there will be no coverage.

> An example: You give your neighbor's son permission to run an errand with your car, telling him that the keys are under the floor mat. Three weeks later, he uses the car without your permission while you are away from home and causes an accident. He would not have coverage.

Disputes over transferring coverage under an auto policy from one person to another are a common source of insurance lawsuits. As a result, insurance companies have drafted detailed definitions of how and when you can transfer coverage to someone else. In short, this isn't very easy to do.

> Your rights and duties under this policy may not be assigned without our written consent. However, if a named insured shown in the Declarations dies, coverage will be provided for:
>
> 1. The surviving spouse if resident in the same household at the time of death. Coverage applies to the spouse as if a named insured shown in the Declarations; and
>
> 2. The legal representative of the deceased person as if a named insured shown in the Declarations. This applies only with respect

to the representative's legal responsibility to maintain or use "your covered auto."

Since the premium charged for some auto coverages is affected by facts about you (such as your driving record, age, use of the car for business or pleasure), the insurance company restricts the transfer of coverages under the policy from the named insured to another person (about whom they do not know) without the company's prior written consent.

Coverage for a legal representative of a deceased person only applies while acting in the capacity of a legal representative with respect to use of a covered auto.

No rights or duties of the insured may be transferred without consent of the company; however, if the named insured dies, the spouse and legal representative of the deceased insured become named insureds under the policy until expiration of the policy.

Employees aren't covered by standard personal auto policies. But there is an exception for one kind of employee—a domestic employee for whom workers compensation benefits are neither required nor available. For most people, this usually means a maid, housekeeper or nanny.

An injury to a domestic employee may be covered by personal auto liability coverage if no workers compensation benefits apply.

IMPORTANT DEFINITIONS

In some states, people who hire domestic employees (including gardeners, chauffeurs, etc.) are required by law to purchase **workers' compensation** coverage to pay for injuries to their employees while on the job. In other states, the coverage is not required, but employers may voluntarily purchase the coverage (in which case the auto insurance benefits aren't available).

This section of the policy also addresses **subrogation** (although indirectly—other sections deal with the matter more directly).

Subrogation involves the substitution of an insurance company to **the rights of a policyholder** because of the company's pre-existing duty to pay the policyholder for a covered loss.

> An example: You're injured in an auto accident that's another driver's fault. Your insurance company has a duty to pay your medical bills as they accumulate and then seek reimbursement from whatever settlement you eventually get from the at-fault driver.

Subrogation disputes often occur **between insurance companies.** One company will battle another over who should pay claims. But these disputes should not directly affect you, as a policyholder making a claim.

A last note on who's covered—or not covered. The standard auto policy includes a **No Benefit to Bailee** paragraph which reads:

CHAPTER 4

> This insurance shall not directly or indirectly benefit any carrier or other bailee for hire.

A bailee is someone who has been entrusted with someone else's property, usually for the purpose of service, repair or storage. Dry cleaners, television repair shops, garages and public parking lots are examples of bailees. These types of businesses can usually be held legally liable for damage to customers' property while it is in their care and possession, and they should purchase liability insurance designed for their exposure as bailees.

An example of the bailee clause: You have your car in a service garage for a new transmission. The work is almost completed when a fire occurs and destroys the car. The company will pay you for the value of the auto, but will not pay the garage (bailee) for the value of the new transmission nor for the labor expended installing it.

WHEN COVERAGE APPLIES

Other than the who, what and when information offered by the Declarations Page and definitions section of the standard form, the most important contractual terms of an insurance policy have to do with when coverage applies.

IMPORTANT DEFINITIONS

The phrase **your covered auto** also applies to several other particular circumstances. The most important of these: When you buy or lease a new car that either replaces a car you used to have or comes in addition to your existing car or cars.

Usually, **physical damage coverage** will apply to **newly acquired vehicles** (whether additional or replacement vehicles) only if you request the coverage within 30 days of the acquisition. However, **liability coverage** for a replacement vehicle is automatically provided until the end of the policy period.

The **liberalization clause** states that if the insurance company makes a change to its policy form which provides broader coverage without a premium charge (for example, if it drops a policy exclusion), that change will automatically apply to your policy on the date the change goes into effect in the insured's state. This simply eliminates the need of the insurance company to endorse all existing policies when coverage is expanded without a change in premium.

Cancellation is an important issue. In most states, the reasons for which an insurance company is permitted to cancel a policy are limited—if the policy has been in effect for at least 60 days or is a renewal policy.

The **general agreement** is a very brief statement. It means simply that all of the remaining provisions of the contract (the policy terms) apply. The reason that the general agreement is so brief is that each coverage section contains a much more detailed insuring agreement.

Although a number of causes of loss are listed and

specifically identified as being other than collision (OTC) losses, nothing in the standard policy says that these are the only covered causes of loss.

This OTC coverage is actually broader than so-called named peril coverage because it also applies to all direct losses which are **not otherwise excluded** by the policy. And a number of exclusions do apply.

EXCLUSIONS

Exclusions involve some of the most heated—and most often litigated—disputes over insurance language.

Some exclusions exist simply to remove coverage for **above-average risk factors** which are not anticipated in average rates and premiums, and that the coverage is often available for an additional charge.

This is the case with respect to **audio, visual and data equipment** and the tapes, records, and **other media** used with such equipment. The basic policy form excludes coverage because these are items of value which have an above-average exposure to theft losses (they are easily removed and are often targets for thieves).

On the other hand, some people want specific drivers excluded from coverage. These special exclusions have become increasingly common in recent years. The 1994 Michigan case *Lynn McMillan v. Auto Club Insurance Association* considered the issue of a **named driver exclusion** to an auto policy.

McMillan owned a 1989 Dodge Ram van and was insured under a no-fault automobile insurance policy

IMPORTANT DEFINITIONS

issued by the Auto Club. At the time in question, McMillan lived with Mervin Carl Timmerman, who had a poor driving record and had previously been involved in an accident with one of McMillan's cars.

In exchange for a lower premium, McMillan obtained a policy from the Auto Club with a named-driver exclusion that excluded Timmerman as a driver of the insured vehicle. The named-driver exclusion provided that various coverages, including comprehensive and collision, would be void and of no effect if the vehicle were operated by Timmerman.

The insurance policy issued to McMillan contained the following provision:

> When a named excluded person operates a vehicle all liability coverage is void—no one is insured. Owners of the vehicle and others legally responsible for the acts of the named excluded person remain fully personally liable.
>
> Soon after the policy was written, Timmerman drove McMillian's van without permission. He caused an accident—which the Auto Club refused to cover.

The trial court sided with McMillan, ruling that coverage was available because the vehicle had been stolen. The Auto Club appealed.

The court ruled that reasonable expectation would have a lot to do with which interpretation it would choose. It would favor McMillan's version—that the exclusion only applied if permission were given—particularly in light of the fact that exclusionary clauses are construed strictly against the insurer.

Most named driver exclusions pertain to **members of your household** whose driving records are so bad that they would make insurance prohibitively expensive.

> Whether they include named driver exclusions or not, issues of household membership are another key cause of coverage disputes.

The somewhat subjective term **social unit** may define who's a member of your household and who isn't.

"In reading the provisions of the policy, we believe that a **reasonable insured** would expect that if the named excluded driver were allowed to operate the vehicle then the various coverages would be void," the court wrote. "However, we also believe that a reasonable insured would also expect that if the vehicle were stolen, even if stolen by a named excluded driver, then there would be coverage under the policy."

> In other words, the policy put McMillan on notice that he wasn't to allow Timmerman to drive the van. But it didn't say he was without coverage if Timmerman took the van without permission.

The court ruled that "assuming that insurers may exclude from coverage claims arising from theft by named excluded drivers, the excluded-driver provision must **incorporate specifically** language that notifies the insured that the exclusion applies even in the event of theft by the named excluded driver."

The excluded-driver provision in McMillan's policy did not exclude specifically coverage where there was a theft by the named excluded driver. McMillan was entitled to coverage if the vehicle were stolen by the named excluded driver.

Most policies include an exclusion for racing injuries. There is no coverage for an insured person while occupying a vehicle located inside a racing facility for the purpose of competing in, or preparing or practicing for, a prearranged or organized race or speed contest.

CONCLUSION

We'll consider more definitions throughout the course of this book. The object of this chapter has been to consider a few of the most basic definitions and show how they impact the mechanics of auto insurance coverage.

CHAPTER 5

WHY LIABILITY IS AN IMPORTANT ISSUE

Liability is probably the most important kind of automobile insurance. It covers moneys owed when one automobile driver causes bodily injury to another person or damage to another person's property.

Injury or damage suffered by a driver who causes an accident is not a matter of legal liability. Being *liable* means being **legally responsible** for damages suffered by a third party (someone other than the driver or owner of the vehicle).

If a driver who causes injury or damage suffered by another person can be shown to be at fault, that driver may be held liable for the accident.

In other words, if you cause an accident, you can't hold yourself liable for injuries you suffer. Anyone else who suffers injuries can hold you liable.

> Technically, liability coverage applies only when you have been found legally liable for injury or damage. The fact that injury or damage has occurred does not necessarily mean that you are legally liable—no matter what an angry driver or his angry lawyer says.

In liability issues, you'll often see or hear references to **first party** and **third party**. In most cases, the first party means the insurance policyholder at fault in an accident—for the sake of illustration, assume this means you—and the third party is the other driver involved in the accident.[1]

First party liabilities—that is, damage you do to yourself and your own property—are relatively easy for insurance companies to calculate and control. Third party liabilities are far more difficult to predict.

If one driver is liable for an accident, then the other party may be entitled to compensation for injuries or damage or both. Compensation may be in the form of money paid to the injured party for **tangible damages** (such as a medical bill or the cost to repair a damaged vehicle) and/or money paid for **intangible damages** (such as pain and suffering).

The intangibles are a big reason for the tremendous sums often awarded in bodily injury liability cases. When you damage another car, your liability might be limited to the value of the vehicle. But if you injure a person in that car, causing a permanent disability and pain and suffering which prevents the person from

---

[1] For the curious, the *second party* refers to your insurance company.

earning a living, courts can award millions of dollars in damages.

Some insurance industry analysts attribute as much as three-quarters of the increase in the cost of auto insurance during the 1980s and 1990s to intangible damages liabilities. They are a big reason for the push for **tort reform** that dominated the political and public policy agenda during the early 1990s.

> The term tort refers to the legal concept of liability for civil damages. It's unrelated to criminal charges—which might result from the same incident. A tortfeasor is the person who causes damages to another's body or property. The tortfeasor is the person who needs liability insurance.

HOW LIABILITY COVERAGE WORKS

Basic limits are the smallest amounts of coverage that are written in your state. In many cases, you will want higher limits of protection.

> It's important to know the basic limits of a policy when comparing premiums quoted by different insurance companies.

Automobile liability coverage consists of **bodily injury** liability and **property damage** liability. The Personal

WHY LIABILITY IS AN IMPORTANT ISSUE

Auto Policy is usually written with a single limit of liability per accident, which is sometimes referred to as a **combined single limit**. It is the maximum amount that the insurance company is obligated to pay for all damages arising out of a single accident.

For example, if a policy is written with a **single limit of liability** of $300,000 per accident, the insurance company will pay up to $300,000 for all bodily injuries and property damage arising out of one accident, regardless of the **number of persons injured**, and regardless of what portion of the loss is bodily injury and what portion is property damage.

Some insurance companies issue automobile policies with split limits of liability coverage, and many of the companies that usually write single limits will provide split limits on request.

> When limits are split, two different limits apply to bodily injury coverage, and a separate limit applies to property damage.

A state might require that automobile owners maintain liability insurance in the following amounts:

- $15,000 per person and $30,000 per accident for claims stemming from **bodily injury,** and
- $10,000 per accident for claims stemming from **property damage**.

Split limits are frequently expressed as three numbers separated by slash marks. The first two numbers represent the bodily injury limits in thousands of dollars, and the third number represents the property damage limit in thousands of dollars. For example, 25/50/5 means $25,000 of bodily injury coverage for each person and $50,000 maximum coverage for all persons injured in one accident, and $5,000 of property damage coverage per accident.

One example: Washington State's minimum liability coverage is 25/50/10, meaning a car owner must have at least $25,000 of coverage for injury to one person, at least $50,000 for injury to two or more people per accident and a minimum of $10,000 for property damage per accident.

> Most experts recommend buying bodily injury coverage of at least $100,000 per person and $300,000 per accident and property damage coverage of at least $25,000. If you have substantial assets to protect—a house or investments—you'll probably want coverage of at least $100,000 and $300,000.

For most people in most situations, split limits are the most economical way to carry sufficient liability coverage.

The Declarations for a standard Personal Auto Policy are set up to reflect a single limit of liability. This means that the policy has separate limits of liability for bodily injury and for property damage.

The bodily injury limit is usually further split into a limit **per person** and a higher limit **per accident**.

If the policy has a single limit of liability, and the accident occurs in a state where the vehicle laws require separate limits of liability, the company will separate the limits to comply with the law, but doing so shall not increase the policy limits.

In a case in which the insured had the split limits shown above, and in which the insured was liable for both bodily injury and property damage in an accident, the most the insurance company would pay would be $35,000.

OTHER FORMS OF LIABILITY COVERAGE

The average person usually carries $25,000 per person per accident in liability. If you live in a high-cost market—including almost every big city—and you need more than minimum amounts of liability insurance, you may be able to slash your auto insurance bill by hundreds of dollars with a **personal liability umbrella policy**—called *plup* in industry lexicon.

Plups are **stand-alone insurance policies** that supplement most other liability insurance you may have purchased. Typically, one umbrella policy would boost the liability protection on your homeowners, auto and—if you have them—boat or vacation home policies.

The average umbrella policy adds $1 million in liability insurance **on top of other insurance** coverages you have. In other words, if your auto policy offers $100,000 in liability protection and your homeowners liability limit is $300,000, one umbrella policy would boost your auto to $1.1 million and your homeowners to $1.3 million.

> The umbrella policy doesn't help you if the house or car is destroyed in a fire or flood. It only kicks in when you're sued. That's why it's fairly cheap, ranging in cost from about $100 to $300 a year.

Some states allow you to agree to give up certain rights to sue in an accident. In return for selecting this **limited tort** option, you receive a state-mandated **premium discount** (usually at least 15 percent).

> Before you choose limited tort coverage, you should understand what that decision could mean. Under the option, you agree to relinquish your right to sue for pain and suffering in the case of a minor injury.

You keep the right to sue, however, if you are **injured seriously**. And you're allowed to sue for damages regardless of the type of injury if you are hit by a **drunken driver, uninsured** or **out-of-state motorist**. In all instances, you retain your right to sue for unpaid medical bills, lost wages and out-of-pocket expenses.

LIABILITY FROM THE INSURANCE COMPANY'S PERSPECTIVE

If you have an auto accident and are legally responsible for bodily injury or property damage, the insurance company will pay for many costs related to that liability. The **insuring agreement** is the part of the standard policy that outlines when and how the company will pay.

> We will pay damages for "bodily injury" or "property damage" for which any "insured" becomes legally responsible because of an auto accident. Damages include prejudgment interest awarded against the "insured." We will settle or defend, as we consider appropriate, any claim or suit asking for these damages. In addition to our limit of liability, we will pay all defense costs we incur. Our duty to settle or defend ends when our limit of liability for this coverage has been exhausted. We have no duty to defend any suit or settle any claim for "bodily injury" or "property damage" not covered under this policy.

The **limit of liability** shown on the policy is the most the company will pay as a result of one accident. This maximum amount is not increased because there is more than one insured or vehicle on the policy, nor is it increased because of the number of claims made or the number of vehicles involved in the accident.

The limit of liability on the policy is the maximum that will be paid by the company as the result of one accident and is not increased by the number of covered persons, the number of claims made, the number of vehicles shown on the policy, or the number of vehicles involved in the accident.

Amounts otherwise payable will usually be reduced by amounts paid or payable for the same injury on behalf of any person legally responsible for the injury (including any direct payments, any payments under other liability policies, and any amounts payable under the liability section or other sections, plus any amounts payable under workers' compensation or disability benefits laws).

> **An example:** A salesperson is involved in an accident with an uninsured motorist and, in the absence of other payments or benefits, would have been entitled to $25,000 in compensatory damages under her uninsured motorists coverage. If the other driver voluntarily pays $4,000 out of personal savings toward her injuries, and her employer provides a total of $11,000 in workers compensation medical and disability benefits, her own insurance company would only be obligated to pay $10,000 under its uninsured motorists coverage.

LIABILITY LIMITS AND SET-OFFS

One issue that comes up often, in the wake of an accident: How will the insurance company **divide a certain liability limit** between two people making claims against a single at-fault driver from a single accident?

WHY LIABILITY IS AN IMPORTANT ISSUE

> To be more specific: If your liability limit is $100,000 per accident and there are two other cars involved in an accident you caused, how will each of those drivers' claims be settled?

The insurance company will give each claimant a **share of the limit of liability proportionate** to his or her claim in relation to the total of all claims submitted.

> To answer the specific question: If one driver claims $60,000 in liability damages and the other claims $90,000, the insurance company will give each a proportional part of the $100,000 limit—$40,000 and $60,000, respectively. They'll have to sue you directly for the rest of their claims.

A more common conflict affecting coverage limits: **set-off provisions** that limit one kind of coverage when another has been claimed.

The 1990 Nevada supreme court decision *Karen Ellison v. California State Automobile Association* considered the insurance company's medical payments set-off—which is supposed to prevent a double payment of medical expenses when claims are made under an auto policy.

Karen Ellison was insured under an automobile insurance policy from respondent California State Automobile Association (CSAA). The policy provided both medical payments coverage and uninsured motorists coverage which included a medical payments provision within it. Separate premiums were assessed for each of the two coverages.

The uninsured motorists coverage provided a setoff provision coordinating the two coverages which stated:

> If an insured person has valid and collectible automobile medical payments insurance available to him, the damages which he shall be entitled to recover from the owner or operator of an uninsured motor vehicle shall be reduced for purposes of uninsured motorists coverage by the amounts paid or due to be paid under such automobile medical payments insurance.

A similar clause was included in the medical payments provision of the policy. It provided:

> Any amount paid or payable for medical expenses under the Liability or Uninsured Motorists coverages of this policy shall be deducted from the amount payable under this part.

Ellison was injured in an accident with an uninsured motorist and incurred medical expenses. CSAA paid the medical expenses under the medical payments portion of the policy. The uninsured motorist claim subsequently went to arbitration and the arbitrator awarded Ellison $10,617.96. This award included $7,000 for pain and suffering and $3,617.96 for medical expenses. CSAA paid the pain and suffering award but, asserting the medical payments setoff provision in the policy, refused to pay the amount awarded for the medical expenses. It claimed that under the setoff provision Ellison was entitled to only one payment of medical expenses which CSAA had already paid.

Ellison sued the CSAA to recover the remainder of the arbitrator's award. The District Court in Clark County granted CSAA's motion for summary judgment. Ellison appealed.

The issue in the appeal was whether a medical payments setoff or crediting provision contained in an automobile insurance policy was enforceable. If so, it would prevent an insured from recovering twice for medical payments under separate provisions of the policy which independently provided medical payments recovery for personal injuries.

The state high court concluded:

> Recovery by [Ellison] in excess of 100 percent of damages is a windfall which will not be countenanced by the court absent clear agreement providing such coverage....The parties' contract unambiguously provides for only one payment of medical expenses if there is overlapping coverage and such expenses result from an accident with an uninsured motorist.

Eight years earlier, the same court had defined its position on liability set-offs. In the 1982 Nevada supreme court decision *Sullivan v. Dairyland Insurance Co.,* an insured's passenger sustained physical injuries that were far in excess of the driver's liability coverage. The passenger sought to collect both the liability and the medical payments coverage from the insurer.

Dairyland relied on a set off clause that allowed it to deduct medical expenses from the uninsured motorist insurance payment. The state supreme court determined that the passenger could recover under both coverages despite the set off clause because "...the set-off clause only operates to prevent double recovery for the same elements of damage...."

The court concluded that although the set off limitation was in keeping with the reasonable expectations of the policyholder, it was inapplicable when the damages exceeded the coverage limits.

CONCLUSION

Liability is the most important reason most people buy auto insurance. If you cause an accident, the damage you can do to another person's car is usually limited. The damage you can do to that person, however, is essentially unlimited.

But, when you're reviewing or comparing auto insurance policies, remember that the word *liability* has different meanings for different parties. For you, it's a potentially unlimited downside you want to limit. For the insurance company, it's the obligation taken on when issuing an insurance policy.

So, the term *limit of liability* which occurs throughout the standard auto policy relates to the insurance company's obligations to you—not your protection against civil lawsuits.

WHY LIABILITY IS AN IMPORTANT ISSUE

The limit of liability is the point at which the insurance company stops paying. If you face potential losses larger than this limit—or if you have assets worth more—you may want to buy higher limits or additional policies that offer umbrella liability protection.

CHAPTER 6

WHY UNINSURED MOTORISTS COVERAGE IS IMPORTANT

Uninsured motorists coverage (often called UM) is designed to protect you for bodily injuries when those injuries are caused by another driver who either has no liability insurance or has coverage which is less than the minimum requirements of state law. UM coverage also protects you for bodily injury when caused by a **hit-and-run driver** who cannot be identified.

> Uninsured motorists are a bigger risk than many people think. According to the California Department of Insurance, in certain parts of Los Angeles County nine out of 10 drivers don't have auto insurance. The same study found that almost **28 percent of all California drivers are uninsured**—that number seems to stay pretty constant in states with the biggest populations.

Even in states which strictly enforce auto insurance rules, uninsured motorists go to great lengths to stay on the road. Some purchase **temporary insurance** to obtain license and inspection seals, then discontinue their payments; others use **counterfeit** insurance cards.

HOW UNINSURED MOTORISTS COVERAGE WORKS

UM coverage was conceived as a partial solution to the problem created by drivers who would not or could not obtain liability insurance. It benefits those who are covered by a Personal Auto Policy under which the insured has purchased UM coverage. It does not benefit the uninsured motorist who is responsible for an accident.

In its 1990 decision *Cynthia Kuda v. American Family Mutual Insurance Co.*, the Missouri Supreme Court considered the limits of liability that an insurance company must meet in uninsured motorists coverage.

Adolph Kuda bought automobile insurance for himself and his family, including his daughter Cynthia, from American Family. The policy contained provisions for injuries incurred as a result of negligence of an uninsured motorist. The policy also included medical expense coverage for Cynthia up to the amount of $2,000.

Cynthia was injured in a collision with an uninsured motorist. As a result of the accident, Cynthia incurred medical expenses of more than $1,700. Cynthia and American Family settled for a payment in the amount of $5,500 under the uninsured motorists coverage. By handwritten provision, Cynthia agreed that:

> This release specifically excludes any claim for payments under the medical pay provision of the above policy.

Cynthia and her attorney accepted and endorsed a check from American Family and returned the release.

A short time later, Cynthia sued American Family, seeking recovery of her $1,700 medical expenses under the medical payments coverage of the policy. American Family asked the trial court to dismiss Cynthia's charges, based on a limitation of liability provision in the medical payments coverage. The company denied having agreed to Cynthia's medical payments exclusion.

The trial court granted American Family's request and dismissed the lawsuit. Kuda appealed.

The Missouri Supreme Court acknowledged that the liability limit became an issue only when a policyholder was involved in an accident with an uninsured motorist. If Cynthia had been involved in a single car accident, the medical expense coverage would be available. Had she been involved in an accident with an insured motorist, American Family would pay the medical expenses.

The high court acknowledged that "The limitation clause upon which American Family relies to deny medical pay coverage is ambiguous."

Its conclusion: In order to establish a level of protection equivalent to the liability coverage a policyholder would have received if involved in an accident with an insured motorist, the insurance company had to pay medical expense up front.

It reversed the lower court's ruling and ordered a judgment in favor of Cynthia Kuda on her claim for medical expenses.

The UM coverage section of the standard auto insurance policy consists of five sections: Insuring Agreement, Exclusions, Limit of Liability, Other Insurance and Arbitration. We'll consider the most important of these briefly.

INSURING AGREEMENT

> A. We will pay compensatory damages which an "insured" is legally entitled to recover from the owner or operator of an "uninsured motor vehicle" because of "bodily injury":
>
> 1. Sustained by an "insured"; and
>
> 2. Caused by an accident.
>
> The owner's or operator's liability for these damages must arise out of the ownership, maintenance or use of the "uninsured motor vehicle."
>
> Any judgment for damages arising out of a suit brought without our written consent is not binding on us.

Section A of the Insuring Agreement describes when the insurance company will pay UM benefits for accidents.

If you sustain injuries as a result of an accident involving an uninsured motor vehicle, the company will pay the amount you're legally entitled to recover from the owner or operator of the uninsured vehicle subject to the limit of insurance. Note that the policy pays *compensatory* damages only. This means it will not pay other damages, such as **punitive damages**.

In most states, UM coverage applies only to bodily injury. Only a handful of states allow this coverage to apply to property damage.

Uninsured motorists coverage pays for injury to you or your passengers caused by an uninsured or a **hit-and-run driver**. It also includes **underinsured motorists** coverage, which makes up the difference between how much you can collect from someone else's insurance and your actual losses.

In order for an injured person to bring suit for damages against the uninsured owner or operator, the written consent of the insurance company must be obtained; otherwise, the insurance company is not bound by a judgment resulting from the suit.

> B. "Insured" as used in this Part means:
>
> 1. You or any "family member."
>
> 2. Any other person "occupying" "your covered auto."
>
> 3. Any person for damages that person is entitled to recover because of "bodily injury" to which this coverage applies sustained by a person described in 1. or 2. above.

This section of the Insuring Agreement defines who is an *insured person* with respect to uninsured motorists coverage.

An *insured* includes the named insured or any family member as occupants of any auto or as pedestrians. It also means a covered auto. Coverage would also extend to a person entitled to recover damages because of injuries to another person. Examples of this would be a loss of consortium (companionship) of a spouse, or medical expenses incurred by the parent of an injured child.

> C. "Uninsured motor vehicle" means a land motor vehicle or trailer of any type:
>
> 1. To which no bodily injury liability bond or policy applies at the time of the accident.
>
> 2. To which a bodily injury liability bond or policy applies at the time of the accident. In this case its limit for bodily injury liability must be less than the minimum limit for bodily injury liability specified by the financial responsibility law of the state in which "your covered auto" is principally garaged.
>
> 3. Which is a hit-and-run vehicle whose operator or owner cannot be identified....
>
> 4. To which a bodily injury liability bond or policy applies at the time of the accident but the bonding or insuring company:
>
> a. denies coverage; or
>
> b. is or becomes insolvent.

This section defines the term "uninsured motor vehicle." However, note that the definition of "uninsured motor vehicle" may vary from state to state by the use of an **amendatory endorsement**.

Several caveats: Vehicles owned or furnished for the regular use of a family member, owned or operated by a self-insurer, or owned by a governmental unit are not to be considered uninsured motor vehicles (but a vehicle owned or operated by a self-insurer which becomes insolvent is considered to be an uninsured vehicle). Also, vehicles operated on rails or treads, those designed for use off public roads (but not while being operated on public roads), or vehicles situated for use as residence premises (e.g., motor homes) are not uninsured motor vehicles.

EXCLUSIONS

A. We do not provide Uninsured Motorists Coverage for "bodily injury" sustained:

1. By an "insured" while "occupying," or when struck by, any motor vehicle owned by that "insured" which is not insured for this coverage under this policy. This includes a trailer of any type used with that vehicle.

2. By any "family member" while "occupying," or when struck by, any motor vehicle you own which is insured for this coverage on a primary basis under any other policy.

B. We do not provide Uninsured Motorists Coverage for "bodily injury" sustained by any "insured":

WHY UNINSURED MOTORISTS COVERAGE IS IMPORTANT

> 1. If that person or the legal representative settles the "bodily injury" claim without our consent.
>
> 2. While "occupying" "your covered auto" when it is being used as a public or livery conveyance. This exclusion (B.2) does not apply to a share-the-expense car pool.
>
> 3. Using a vehicle without a reasonable belief that that "insured" is entitled to do so....

There are **fewer exclusions** in the uninsured motorists section of the policy than in other coverage sections. Five situations are described under which there is no coverage for an insured person's bodily injury.

Uninsured Motorists Coverage is not provided for:

- Any person occupying or struck by a vehicle which is owned by you or a family member for which uninsured motorists coverage is not provided under the policy. Also, there is no coverage for a trailer being used with such a vehicle.

- Any family member occupying or struck by a vehicle you own but which is covered under another insurance policy.

- Any injured person who settles a bodily injury claim without the consent of the company.

- Any person occupying a covered auto while it is being used to transport persons or property for a fee, except for a car pool for the purpose of sharing expenses.

- Any person using a vehicle who does not have a reasonable belief of being entitled to do so.

To the extent that any payment under this coverage would reduce amounts otherwise payable under any **workers compensation** or **disability** law, the uninsured motorists coverage will not apply.

This section reinforces the Insuring Agreement, which says that the coverage only applies to "compensatory" damages. This exclusion makes it clear that uninsured motorists coverage does not apply to "punitive or exemplary" damages.

The **limits of liability** for UM coverage usually have a single-limit, which is often lower than limits for bodily injury or damage that you do to other drivers. Since UM covers first party losses, you can project how much coverage you would need to replace damage you might sustain.

The **other insurance** clause for UM coverage differs from the provisions that apply to other coverages. The first provision states that any recovery under all policies or UM coverages may not exceed the **highest applicable limit** for any one vehicle. This makes it clear that stacking of limits is not intended or permitted.

The second provision relates to non-owned vehicles. Any UM insurance provided with respect to a non-owned vehicle will be provided on an excess basis if the other insurance is provided on a primary basis.

The final provision of the UM other insurance section states that insurance will be shared proportionally, based on limits, when two or more policies provide coverage.

ARBITRATION

>Both parties must agree to arbitration. If so agreed, each party will select an arbitrator. The two arbitrators will select a third. If they cannot agree within 30 days, either may request that selection be made by a judge of a court having jurisdiction.
>
>...Unless both parties agree otherwise, arbitration will take place in the county in which the "insured" lives. Local rules of law as to procedure and evidence will apply. A decision agreed to by two of the arbitrators will be binding as to:
>
>1. Whether the "insured" is legally entitled to recover damages; and
>
>2. The amount of damages. This applies only if the amount does not exceed the minimum limit for bodily injury liability specified by the financial responsibility law of the state in which "your covered auto" is principally garaged. If the amount exceeds that limit, either party may demand the right to a trial. This demand must be made within 60 days of the arbitrators' decision. If this demand is not made, the amount of damages agreed to by the arbitrators will be binding.

The final section in the UM coverage portion of the policy is titled "Arbitration." **Arbitration** means negotiation by impartial persons when you and your insurance company cannot agree on settling an uninsured motorists claim. Disagreement might concern whether you are legally entitled to recover damages or might concern the amount of recovery.

> If you and the insurance company do not agree that you have a valid claim, or disagree as to the amount of the claim, both sides must agree to arbitration. Each party selects an arbitrator, and they select a third arbitrator. Each party pays the cost of its own arbitrator and splits the cost of the third arbitrator.

Arbitration usually takes place in the county in which you live and **the decision is binding as to the entitlement of damages and the amount, unless the amount** exceeds that required by financial responsibility laws, in which case either party may demand the right to a trial.

UNDERINSURED MOTORISTS COVERAGE

Underinsured motorists coverage applies when another driver who causes an accident has liability insurance, but the insurance that driver has is inadequate to cover resulting injuries.

> For example: You carry $50,000 of underinsured motorists coverage. Another driver swerves onto the wrong side of the street and hits your car head-on. You need $45,000 to cover your injuries. The other driver only has $30,000 of bodily injury liability coverage and cannot personally pay the additional damages. The other driver's insurance company would pay you $30,000 and the "underinsured" motorists component of your coverage would pay the additional $15,000.

Underinsured motorists coverage is often **linked directly with UM coverage** in a standard policy. However these coverages appear, it's usually a good idea to make sure they offer coverage limits in line with the other property coverage in the policy.

A series of state court rulings in the early 1990s eliminated many of the **liability limits** for uninsured and underinsured motorists coverage—especially in fatal accidents. As a result, many insurance companies increased their cash reserves against UM claims.

In 1994, the Ohio Insurance Institute estimated that the changes in UM claims would result in rates on uninsured and underinsured motorists coverage doubling. Many people in the insurance industry worried that such a spike would convince some drivers to drop the coverage.

> With something like one in four drivers not carrying auto insurance, dropping UM coverage is not a good idea.

CONCLUSION

Because a disturbing number of drivers—especially those in urban areas—don't have insurance, uninsured motorists coverage is an important component of any auto insurance package.

While most states don't require UM coverage, auto finance and leasing companies will almost always insist on the coverage as a prerequisite. And going without doesn't make much sense. In most situations, UM coverage isn't expensive—and its cost isn't affected by your driving record or other variable factors.

WHY UNINSURED MOTORISTS COVERAGE IS IMPORTANT

CHAPTER 7

HOW NO-FAULT INSURANCE WORKS

A favorite auto insurance topic among consumer advocates and some regulators is **the no-fault system**. Some states have enacted various versions of no-fault auto insurance. In 1995, thirteen states used some form of no-fault. What this means and how it affects the insurance you buy requires some explanation.

> There are no-fault elements to all auto insurance policies. The medical payments and property damage sections of the collision coverage will pay, no matter who was responsible for an accident. No-fault systems take this element to a higher level.

Supporters say that no-fault promises **quicker payment** of insurance claims, because there's no wait for insurance companies—or courts—to decide who's to blame for an accident. A growing number of insurance companies agree, saying that no-fault systems reduce their costs—and the resulting higher auto insurance premiums—**by limiting the number of lawsuits** over auto insurance policies.

> That's a big plus for an insurance sector in which legal fees account for 12 percent of premium costs, while medical expenses account for 15 percent.

The basic factors that shape no-fault programs include:

- **Thresholds**: Designers of a no-fault system must decide when injuries are so severe that a person should be allowed to sue the driver responsible. Make the threshold too low, and people will flock to court; too high, and some might not be fairly compensated. Most no-fault proponents favor a verbal threshold that spells out which specific injuries permit a trip to court. The alternative is a monetary threshold, which allows lawsuits for damages above a specified amount. But detractors are concerned this encourages the padding of medical bills to exceed the threshold.

- **Benefit (or liability) limits**: What are the maximum benefits an injured motorist can receive under a no-fault policy? While some suggest a limit as high as

$250,000, the industry proposal puts the cap on benefits at $50,000, which insurance officials say covers 97 percent of all auto claims.

- **Lost coverage allowances**: No-fault can mean that drivers pay more to maintain their current level of coverage. For instance, since no-fault only covers insured motorists and their passengers, a driver might have to buy a separate liability policy to cover such things as hitting a parked car.

- **Cost containment**: Low-cost policies also could require medical treatment from a managed-care provider.

"PURE" NO-FAULT

One reason proponents defend no-fault so staunchly is that when they say *no-fault*, they generally mean **pure no-fault**.

Under a pure no-fault system, virtually all lawsuits related to auto accidents are eliminated. The right to sue and a chance for a damage award are replaced with the right to *guaranteed benefits*. Lawsuits are retained only to punish convicted drunken drivers and others guilty of criminal conduct. Policyholders pay premiums to protect themselves. If they (or their passengers) are injured, they are compensated by their own insurers—no matter who caused any part of an accident.

That's unlike a liability system, which requires the responsible party's insurer to pay for medical bills and car repairs.

HOW NO-FAULT INSURANCE WORKS

> There is no pure no-fault system in the United States.

In 1995, the Hawaiian state legislature adopted what would have been the first pure no-fault program. Consumer advocate Ralph Nader visited Hawaii to support the plan.

Nader challenged lawmakers to repeal Hawaii's 21-year-old partial no-fault auto insurance plan, which prohibits lawsuits until medical bills exceed $10,000. He said that a limited reform plan, which would allow lawsuits after damages exceed $20,000 and offer consumers a choice of policies, was too complex. "And complexity always works to the benefit of the auto insurance company against the consumer," he said.

Nader and other supporters said that, under pure no-fault, consumers would no longer have to hope that the person who hit them was rich or well-insured. They wouldn't have to split the settlements with lawyers. Most importantly, they wouldn't have to subsidize uninsured motorists with UM coverage.

Savings would have come largely from eliminating lawsuits except when an accident is the result of a criminal act such as drunken driving, and from shifting the medical costs to the victim's regular health insurance, which state law requires all employers to supply.

But Hawaiian Governor Ben Cayetano said it would cost victims their chance to sue for compensation for

CHAPTER 7

pain and suffering. Cayetano then unveiled his own plan, which would provide every car owner with $25,000 worth of liability insurance and let health insurance pay for traffic-related injuries.

Cayetano's plan would be financed by a 25-cent-per-gallon gasoline surcharge and a $17 increase in motor vehicle registration. Motorists could buy additional coverage and could sue only for serious injuries or death.

> The California-based RAND Institute estimated that the Hawaiian pure no-fault initiative would have provided drivers with $1 million in medical and wage loss coverage for an average of 48 percent less than they paid for less injury coverage under the liability system.

About the same time that the Hawaiian no-fault plan fell into a political bog, a group of high-tech entrepreneurs in California proposed a package of ballot initiatives which included a nearly pure no-fault auto insurance plan. The group called itself the Alliance to Revitalize California (ARC) and positioned its ideas as good for both consumers and businesses.

The ARC no-fault proposal would require that people have minimum insurance policies to register their cars. It also would require that insurance companies pay claims within a month, or pay 2 percent per month interest.

In most cases, policyholders would lose the right to sue over accidents. However, they could sue if an insurance company refused to pay benefits, if the other driver in an accident was under the influence of drugs or alcohol, or if the crash was caused by defects in the car or road hazards.

> Under the ARC proposal, the standard policy would cover up to $1 million in medical and other damages. Drivers could sign waivers to buy smaller policies, and insurance companies would have to offer policies providing coverage of up to $5 million.

PARTIAL NO-FAULT

The ARC program came pretty close to pure no-fault. But most of the no-fault programs currently in place can best be called **partial no-fault**. They allow you to make a claim up to a certain dollar limit without having to determine who caused an accident.

About the same time that ARC was pushing for a pure no-fault system in California, the state's Insurance Commissioner and a group of consumer advocacy groups proposed a partial no-fault alternative.

The plan that Commissioner Chuck Quackenbush supported would have required all drivers to purchase a basic policy with $15,000 in medical and lost wage benefits—for **an annual premium of $220** for most drivers. People injured in an automobile accident would be entitled to compensation for medical bills and lost wages up to the $15,000 limit regardless of who caused an accident. Pain and suffering claims would be limited to those whose injuries were **serious or permanent.**

The minimum policy would be mandatory for all Californians, with proof of insurance required for vehicle registration.

Modeled after New York's no-fault law, it used a **verbal threshold**—"serious or permanent injury"—rather than a financial target to determine in which cases litigation may be pursued.

> In New York, all auto insurance policies must contain $50,000 in no-fault coverage for medical expenses and lost wages. Policies still have liability coverage, but that only begins after the $50,000 no-fault limit has been used up.

A COMMON PROBLEM

Despite their political popularity, partial no-fault have some **technical problems.** A common one: low liability limits like the $50,000 in New York. While most people would consider **low liability limits** a good thing, they can create conflicts.

For example, a person who's been in an accident collects money from the at-fault driver and then makes a claim against his or her own no-fault policy. This is called **double-dipping** (it's similar to cases in which a person injured on the job collects money from a personal health insurance and an employer's workers' comp insurance).

REGULATORY TRENDS

Regulators and politicians can't seem to make up their minds about no-fault auto coverage. Since 1970, **16 states and Puerto Rico** have adopted some form of modified no-fault auto insurance, but four states have repealed their no-fault laws since then. (Pennsylvania adopted no-fault in 1976, repealed it in 1984 and re-enacted a different version in 1990.)

> **Michigan and New York often are cited as having good experiences with no-fault. Georgia and Connecticut, which repealed no-fault in the 1990s, often are cited as having bad experiences with the system.**

Some consumer advocates who support no-fault argue that **trial lawyer groups** spend a lot of money to oppose any form of no-fault. And, even in states which have stuck with no-fault plans, regulators have tended to lower liability limits—which lawyers like.

Under New Jersey's no-fault auto insurance law, all drivers must buy **personal injury protection** (PIP) coverage. If an accident occurs, it pays for all medical bills and lost wages for the insured up to $250,000. Drivers have to buy PIP as part of every automobile insurance policy. This coverage is a substitute for the indemnification typically handled through civil lawsuits.

After meeting with insurance-related interest groups and members of the public in late 1994, New Jersey Insurance Commissioner Drew Karpinski announced that he would seek to provide drivers with more options for **scaling back PIP coverage**—and other auto insurance coverages—in order to lower costs.

In Michigan, legislators consider modifications to the state's expensive no-fault system on what seems like an on-going basis. That state's PIP coverage also has **no liability limit**—although the financial model on which it's based assumes an average limit of $250,000.

> No other no-fault state requires unlimited PIP coverage. New Jersey requires $250,000 and Colorado $200,000. All other states require a limit of $50,000 or less.

The troubling trend for Michigan auto insurance costs is that the total value of so-called "PIP catastrophic" claims, those exceeding $250,000, exploded in the late 1980s and early 1990s. The cost of paid claims rose by more than 1,500 percent between 1984 and 1994, while the number of claims reported rose by about 200 percent.

In insurance industry jargon, this kind of increase is called a **deterioration in claims experience**. As a result of Michigan's deterioration, the annual cost of PIP coverage rose from $3 in 1978 to $23.60 in 1988 to $96.95 in 1995. This is a surcharge added to the premium of every driver in the state.

> Insurers blame Michigan's unlimited benefits for driving up the cost of premiums by more than 50 percent between 1990 and 1995. "If you're going to have a Michigan-style system, you might as well not have no-fault at all," said a spokesman for one of the biggest auto insurance companies in the country.

In 1993, Connecticut abandoned its no-fault system to return to a traditional **liability system**. Repealing the no-fault system wasn't easy but, "considering the alternatives, it was the least Draconian, the least intrusive, the least traumatic impact on the consumers," said Garrett Moore, president of the Connecticut Trial Lawyers Association.

Savings from reform came, in part, by **eliminating stacking** (the practice of combining benefits from coverage on more than one car) and other factors that increased claims. But the savings came primarily from no longer requiring the partial no-fault coverage, which paid up to $5,000 for medical bills and lost wages.

Connecticut Insurance Commissioner Robert Googins noted that rates on policies dropped 7.7 percent on a weighted state average—but the effect on individual consumers varied widely. At some companies, rising costs of liability claims offset cost reductions from reform.

REFORMING NO-FAULT

Some consumer groups defend the traditional liability system because it allows people to win large awards when they're injured. This argument holds that **no-fault systems subsidize the wealthy**—relatively—by limiting all claims.

But defenders of no-fault also champion the poor. Richard Woll, senior actuary at the California-based Allstate Research & Planning Center, believes the traditional liability system is "unfair to poor people, who must purchase insurance to protect the assets of the wealthy."

> Not only do many less-wealthy motorists find auto insurance unaffordable, but they also are the ones who most need the guaranteed prompt payments to cover the costs of their accidents.

The experience of the 13 no-fault states suggests that they haven't been successful in restraining auto-insurance rates. The original concept of waiving the right to sue in return for prompt, guaranteed medical payments fell victim to the lobbying efforts of **trial lawyers**, who insisted on preserving the right to sue, **the medical profession**, which pushed for enriched medical benefits, and **consumer groups**, which wanted both.

Jeffrey O'Connell, a law professor at the University of Virginia, was one of the founding fathers of no-fault insurance. But, during the 1990s, O'Connell became a critic of the system as it currently exists. He argued that his first no-fault model, developed in the mid-1960s, was "bastardized" by state legislators beholden to powerful special interest groups.

O'Connell didn't give up, though. A model he developed in 1994 would give consumers the choice of purchasing no-fault coverage or, for a significantly higher premium, full liability coverage. Those who elect no-fault would **waive the right to sue** for noneconomic damages such as pain and suffering. A PIP policy would cover their economic damages regardless of fault. In return, they would be **insulated from liability** claims by other motorists.

Motorists who retain their right to sue for noneconomic damages would remain in the tort liability system. However, such drivers also would have to purchase **tort maintenance insurance** similar to uninsured motorists coverage.

O'Connell estimates that no-fault choosers would **save from 25 to 40 percent** on their auto insurance bill, depending on the limits chosen and their state of residence.

The RAND Institute, which calculated expected premium reductions under O'Connell's **optional no-fault plan**, projected savings of more than $14 billion for private passenger vehicles alone. The premium rate reductions would be largest for low-income drivers, many of whom are uninsured due to high auto coverage costs.

In addition to lowering the costs of auto insurance, O'Connell claims the proposal offers several other advantages to drivers and insurers. For example, he says, **health care fraud and abuse** would decrease by cutting the link between medical costs and noneconomic cash awards, which generally are calculated as multiples of medical costs.

Under O'Connell's new plan, there would be no incentive for accident victims to run up unnecessary medical bills to qualify for pain and suffering compensation.

> The biggest criticism of O'Connell's new plan: Pennsylvania has an optional no-fault system like the one he proposes—and few people choose the no-fault option.

O'Connell attributes early problems to the "incredibly crude and unsound" way the Pennsylvania program was structured. He says the legislature dictated the rating methodology to be used, which resulted in a 22 percent rate decrease for no-fault drivers and an 11 percent decrease for those electing to retain their tort rights. With **no mechanism for transferring savings** to those who choose no-fault, he says, such motorists do not receive the benefits they deserve for giving up the right to sue.

Also, Pennsylvanians who fail to make a selection are placed in the liability system.

O'Connell says New Jersey's three-year-old choice no-fault is closer to his model but still has a **major structural deficiency** since the people who choose the liability system can sue no-fault drivers. Still, O'Connell notes, "over half the drivers in New Jersey choose no-fault, and our plan offers a much higher level of savings."

CONCLUSION

In theory, no-fault insurance is an appealing alternative to the vicious circle of third-party liability claims, lawsuits and rising premiums that plagues traditional insurance programs.

Unfortunately, the no-fault plans that have been tested so far have had mixed results in practice. No-fault supporters argue that this is because the programs that have been tried are only partial efforts. They argue that, in order to work effectively, a no-fault program would have to prohibit most liability lawsuits.

This issue gets back to a subject we've considered before—and will see again: Liability. The explosion of liability lawsuits that has clogged up the legal system for more than a generation is also responsible for many problems in the insurance industry.

As long as people look at insurance as a means of gaining financial windfalls larger than damages they suffer in auto accidents, no-fault will have trouble being implemented.

CHAPTER 8

HOW ENDORSEMENTS AND OTHER CHANGES WORK

Since an insurance policy is a legal **contract**, you or your insurance company cannot simply take a pen and make changes to the policy. To **change** any portion of the policy (whether the information on the Declarations Page or any of the policy terms and conditions), the insurance company must issue a form that identifies what change is being made. The form is then attached to the policy, and the change becomes binding on both parties.

Forms like this—and the changes that they make—are called **endorsements.**

Additional forms are also attached to a policy to add **optional coverages** that are not included in the standard policy form. These forms may be attached when a policy is first issued, or at a later date.

HOW ENDORSEMENTS AND OTHER CHANGES WORK

> A variety of endorsements may be used in connection with an auto policy. Endorsements may do something as simple as correcting a misspelling of your name or something more complex such as changing the insured vehicles or adding a coverage that is not mentioned in the original policy.

Endorsements may be used to change information in the Declarations, or to add, delete, or modify coverages, exclusions or policy provisions. Although all endorsements change the policy, not all endorsements require a **premium adjustment.**

You'll find the language in most endorsements is very similar to language you see elsewhere in the standard policy. We will not examine every line or every provision in these endorsements, because there are so many of them. Instead, we'll focus on the primary purpose of each form.

You don't need to know every provision and every definition that may appear in these forms. It is more important for you to be aware that these endorsements exist, and to know in general what each one does, and when they are to be used.

> Not all of these endorsements are used by automobile insurers. And some policies may have other conditions required by state law.

CHAPTER 8

CHANGE ENDORSEMENT

Whenever endorsements are attached to the policy at the time the policy is issued, their **endorsement numbers** will be typed on the policy Declarations Page. But when it is necessary to add an endorsement after a policy is in effect, in most cases the **Change Endorsement** must also be issued. The reason for this is that only the Change Endorsement has places for entering the policy number and effective date of the change.

Basically, the Change Endorsement acts something like a **cover letter**, by providing important information about an accompanying endorsement.

> A growing number of insurance companies print their own endorsement forms which include preprinted blanks at the top for indicating policy number, effective date, and so forth. This makes the Change Endorsement unnecessary and the insurance company can issue one piece of paper each time an endorsement is required.

SUSPENSION OF INSURANCE

This endorsement is helpful if you're not going to use one or more covered autos for a lengthy period of time. The Suspension of Insurance endorsement is normally issued after a policy is written. It **temporarily stops coverage** for the car that you're not using.

The Suspension of Insurance endorsement states that **premium will be refunded** if coverage is suspended for at least thirty consecutive days. But it does not have a place to indicate how long the insurance is to be suspended.

For this reason, you have to notify the insurance company when you want coverage to be restored. In most cases, the insurance company will then calculate any refund due and restore coverage by issuing a **Reinstatement endorsement.**

SPLIT LIABILITY LIMITS

The standard Personal Auto Policy is designed to provide liability coverage with a **single limit** of insurance per accident. Optional **split limits** are available with this endorsement.

> Some people prefer split limits because they are more cost-effective than other packages. But, in most cases, split limits are needed to satisfy the minimum requirements of a financial responsibility law or to satisfy requirements for underlying insurance when a Personal Umbrella liability policy is being written.

For whatever reason split limits are requested or required, an endorsement would be attached to the policy to provide them. This form modifies the limit of liability provision by specifying that separate limits apply to **each person** and to **each accident** for bodily injury losses and a separate limit of liability applies to **property damage** losses on a per accident basis.

INCREASED LIMITS TRANSPORTATION EXPENSES

The standard Personal Auto Policy contains a section entitled *Transportation Expenses*. That section describes the conditions under which a policyholder can receive payment for the expenses of **renting a substitute auto** when a covered auto has been damaged or stolen. Policy coverage for transportation expenses begins after a **waiting period**—48 hours in the event of total theft of an auto, and 24 hours after an auto is withdrawn from use due to any other covered loss.

> However, the standard policy coverage is limited to $15 a day and a $450 maximum benefit. In many cities, those limits would be inadequate to cover current rental car costs.

The **Increased Limits Transportation Expenses Coverage** endorsement may be attached to raise the coverage amount to $30 a day and a $900 maximum payment. These higher limits of coverage apply only to covered autos which are described in the schedule and for which **an additional premium** for increased limits is shown.

COVERAGE FOR TAPES, RECORDS, OR OTHER DEVICES

In the standard Personal Auto Policy, various exclusions remove coverage for tapes, records, and other media and accessories used with audio, visual and data equipment. If you keep a number of tapes or compact discs in your car, you might choose to purchase coverage for these items.

> Coverage for this sort of personal property is usually sold with low liability limits for the insurance company—usually less than $500, often less than $250. It's not a great deal of coverage.

This endorsement will be attached to the policy or a Change Endorsement when issued after the policy is written, and an **additional premium** will be charged.

COVERAGE FOR VISUAL AND OTHER MEDIA

The endorsement for tapes and records provides limited coverage for media used with sound equipment and other equipment—but it does not cover the equipment. For example, it would not cover the loss of a two-way radio, car phone or other device.

More complete coverage can be obtained by purchasing the **Coverage for Audio, Visual and Data Electronic Equipment and Tapes, Records, Discs and**

Other Media endorsement. This endorsement covers equipment (such as two-way radios, FAX machines, car phones) as well as media used with such devices.

> In order to be covered, the equipment must either be permanently installed in the auto or be removable from a housing which is permanently installed. It must be designed to be operated solely by the auto's electrical power system. The equipment must receive, transmit or record audio, visual or data signals.

There is no coverage under this endorsement for devices used solely to reproduce sound or that monitor the car's operating system (such devices are covered under the standard coverage—as long as they are permanently installed).

Under this endorsement, coverage for audio, visual and data electronic equipment is written for **a specified dollar amount,** while coverage for tapes, discs and other media is still subject to a lower limit. Losses are paid at the **lowest of three values**: the limit of insurance, the actual cash value or the amount necessary to repair or replace the property.

COVERED PROPERTY COVERAGE

The standard auto policy excludes coverage for the loss of **awnings, cabanas, or equipment** designed to create additional living facilities. Such equipment is often a part of campers and vans.

If you need coverage for these kinds of property, this endorsement can be added to the standard policy for **an additional premium.**

CUSTOMIZING EQUIPMENT COVERAGE

Another exclusion under the standard policy removes coverage for damage to **custom furnishings and equipment,** such as camper kitchen equipment, carpeting, sleeping facilities, and so forth. This is a particular issue for people who drive recreational vehicles and so-called custom van conversions.

If you need coverage for these sorts of furnishings and/or equipment, you can purchase the Customizing Equipment Coverage endorsement for **an additional premium.**

LOSS PAYABLE CLAUSE

As we've noted before, auto purchases are frequently financed through banks or credit companies. When you borrow money to buy a car, both you and the lender have an insurable interest in the car until the loan is paid off. To protect its interest, the lender will usually require that you purchase insurance to cover the auto against theft, damage or other loss. The lender in these cases becomes the **loss payee**.

When you indicate that another party has an insurable interest in a covered auto, the insurance company will usually attach the **Loss Payable Clause** endorsement to the policy. Copies of the policy as well as all endorsements are sent to the loss payee as well as to you.

There is **no additional premium** charged for this endorsement, because it does not change the insurance exposure—it only affects to whom loss settlements will be paid.

ADDITIONAL INSURED—LESSOR

Leasing companies (lessors) are in a similar position to lending companies, in that they have an insurable interest in autos they have leased to their customers.

Since the leasing company remains the **legal owner** of the leased vehicle, it is possible for that company to become legally **liable for injury or damage** involving the leased vehicle. For these reasons, leasing companies usually require that they be included as additional insureds on the policies of people leasing vehicles.

Here, as in the case of Loss Payable Clause, there should be **no additional premium** charged for this endorsement.

COVERAGE FOR DAMAGE TO YOUR AUTO (MAXIMUM LIMIT)

This endorsement is used when you need physical damage coverage for an automobile with an unusual value. Under the standard policy, losses are usually settled on the basis of **actual cash value**. But this can be a problem if you own a unique, custom-made or antique car.

The **value of a collectible car** may be difficult to determine and is not affected by depreciation in the usual manner. The actual cash value of a collector's item vehicle may actually increase with time.

> A policyholder won't usually be satisfied with an ACV settlement based on the make and model year of a car that has special value. But this kind of special value is difficult to calculate. Since the amount of value is difficult to predict accurately, the insurance company does not know what its exposure is nor what to properly charge for the coverage.

One solution to the problem is to write the insurance for these vehicles on a **stated amount basis**. This establishes a maximum value which the insured and insurer agree upon.

An important note: Losses will still be settled on the basis of the lowest of the stated amount, actual cash value, or repair or replacement cost.

> For example, if the cost to repair a partial loss is reasonable, that amount would likely be paid. If, on the other hand, the vehicle is a total loss and cannot be repaired or replaced, and the ACV is difficult to determine, the insurance company would probably pay the stated amount.

MISCELLANEOUS TYPE VEHICLE ENDORSEMENT

The Personal Auto Policy definition of *your covered auto* can be modified by use of the **Miscellaneous Type Vehicle Endorsement**.

CHAPTER 8

> This endorsement form is often used to insure types of vehicles that are not normally eligible for personal auto coverage under a standard policy—like cars not designed for road travel and recreational vehicles.

The endorsement changes the policy definition of *your covered auto* to include miscellaneous type vehicles. It states that a *covered auto* includes any *miscellaneous type vehicle* shown in the schedule or Declarations. It also allows coverage for any miscellaneous type vehicles acquired during the policy period.

The rest of this definition is the same as the definition found in the standard policy (including the requirement to notify the insurance company within 30 days with respect to coverage for additional vehicles, or physical damage coverage for replacement vehicles).

The endorsement contains space for indicating whether the **passenger hazard** is excluded for each insured vehicle. When the *Yes* box is checked, there is no liability coverage under the policy with respect to injuries to a person occupying that miscellaneous type vehicle.

JOINT OWNERSHIP COVERAGE ENDORSEMENT

The **Joint Ownership Coverage** endorsement may be attached to a standard Personal Auto Policy to insure vehicles which normally would not be eligible under the standard ownership rules.

Under the **standard ownership rules**, an eligible vehicle must be owned or leased by an individual or married couple who are residents of the same household. The Joint Ownership Coverage endorsement makes coverage available for vehicles which are owned by individuals other than husband and wife who reside in the same household, and for related individuals who live in different households.

A note: The **Joint Ownership Coverage endorsement** and the **Miscellaneous Type Vehicle Endorsement** may be used to change the ownership rules for eligibility and the types of vehicles eligible for coverage under a standard policy.

CONCLUSION

Making changes to an existing auto insurance policy can be difficult—making changes to any contract usually is. Fortunately, many of the most common changes people need to make have been incorporated into a series of fairly standard policy endorsements.

Some endorsements require additional premiums or fees—but many don't.

These endorsements add or delete cars, people or coverages from insurance policies. They can also raise or lower the coverage limits in a policy. They make these changes in language that the insurance industry and its legal tools can understand.

Endorsements also allow you to adjust a standard insurance policy to your specific needs, without having to get into the expensive and time-consuming process of negotiating a customized policy.

CHAPTER 8

If you need to make a change to a policy that existing endorsements don't address, you can negotiate a custom endorsement.

However you proceed, the purpose of endorsements is to keep as much of the insurance policy as possible in standardized language. This keeps claims-making and settlement confusion to a minimum—which is good for everyone involved.

HOW ENDORSEMENTS AND OTHER CHANGES WORK

CHAPTER 9

TIPS FOR SHOPPING FOR CAR INSURANCE

Once you've got a working knowledge of the elements of an auto insurance policy, you can begin the process of shopping for a new policy—or one to replace the policy you currently have.

The Insurance Information Institute in New York warns against **shopping on price alone.** The group suggests talking to a number of insurers first to get a feeling for the quality of their service.

> Independent insurance agents can help sort through different policies offered by different insurance companies. But you don't have to use an insurance agent or broker. A growing number of auto insurance companies are organized to sell coverage directly—primarily over the telephone. If you know what kind of coverage you need and are willing to spend some time on the phone, you can shop for insurance yourself.

Of course, consumer rights' groups almost always lecture people about comparison shopping for price and service. But they often leave out the specifics of how to make the comparisons.

In this chapter, we'll consider the most important factors that determine how much an auto insurance policy costs. These should also be the main points for comparing policies and quotes offered by different companies.

CONSIDERING INSURANCE COMPANIES

The kind of **insurance company** you choose can make a big difference, especially when you have to make a claim. Different companies stress different specialties—some, low prices...others, excellent service.

Insurers that use **direct marketing** as their main method of selling coverage might be able to offer cheaper premiums—but these price breaks often come at the cost of the level of service other carriers offer.

> Direct marketers don't use agents or brokers to sell their insurance; they sell through direct mail and telemarketing. They usually handle claims in a similar manner. This has become one of the fastest-growing parts of the auto insurance market. It's cheap—but not always strong on customer service.

CHAPTER 9

Other **business priorities** affect the insurance a company offers. If a company only writes policies for squeaky-clean drivers, its rates are going to be lower than one that takes a broader range of drivers, hoping to make money on higher volume. Some companies charge more so they can provide quicker service.

> If an insurance company has more claims adjusters in your area, it will probably settle cases faster. But it will also probably charge more in premiums.

Some insurance companies offer discounts to auto owners who agree to have accident repairs done at preapproved body shops. Insurers say they can save millions on the costs of processing accident claims by virtually eliminating the insurance appraiser. They compare the **cost-containment** plans to managed-care systems in the health insurance market.

> In 1995, only a handful of accident claims fell under cost-containment options. But industry officials predicted that 25 percent of claims would use the systems by the year 2000.

Under cost-containment plans (also called **preferred provider option** plans), repair shops appraise cars and send the estimates to the insurance company via computer. That cuts from 14 days to seven the typical time it takes to get a damaged vehicle repaired. Because the shop gets a steady stream of wrecked cars, the insurance company gets **reduced labor rates and parts discounts**—usually 5 percent to 10 percent.

Preferred provider option is an outgrowth of another plan—called **direct repair programs**—that insurance companies began offering in the late 1980s. Direct repair programs allow owners to choose a body shop recommended by the insurance firm, but the owner also can go to a shop not on the list.

> In Pennsylvania, state approved auto insurance rates dropped between 1993 and 1995 largely due to a cost containment provision in a 1990 reform law.

As with all insurance policies, don't assume all insurance companies will charge the same premium for similar coverage. Depending on where you live and what your driving record is, a service-oriented carrier may charge about the same premium as a no-frills direct marketer.

> Ironically, drivers with bad—but not horrible—driving records sometimes find less difference in the premiums they're quoted than good drivers. Of course, all the quotes will tend to be high.

As a rule of thumb, it's a good idea to ask for premium quotes from at least **three insurance companies** plus your state's assigned risk program (or whatever version of a **state-sponsored program** it uses).

The state program will give you a **baseline for cost and coverage** against which to compare the other policies. This will give you a good chance of eliminating any particularly bad deals.

For example: In 1994, National Insurance Consumer Organization President Robert Hunter said older drivers would probably pay less in their state's **assigned risk insurance plan** than they would paying AARP's heavily-promoted auto insurance. "Guaranteed renewability at unaffordable prices is no guarantee at all," said Hunter—referring to the biggest reason older people buy AARP insurance.

CHARTING OPTIONS

An important point to remember when you're buying auto insurance: Like all coverage, this protection imposes certain **conditions**. Some people—driven by temperament or extreme circumstances—try to control how their cars are repaired after an accident.

It's better to take a more detached view. Buy car insurance that protects your assets and your well-being. Find a company that makes you comfortable you'll be treated in a manner you prefer. Then, if a claim has to be made, focus on **getting what's damaged fixed**.

Don't try to manage your insurance company through the claims process.

TIPS FOR SHOPPING FOR CAR INSURANCE

Before you contact any agents or insurance companies, make a **chart listing the different coverages**—liability, property damage, collision, comprehensive, medical payments, uninsured motorists, etc.—with the amounts of coverage and the deductibles noted. This will help you sort out and compare the quotes and coverages from each company.

Most financial advisers generally recommend that you carry bodily-injury coverage of at least $100,000 per person and $300,000 per accident, as well as property-damage coverage of at least $100,000. If you have substantial net worth that you want to protect against potential lawsuits, you'll want to increase your bodily-injury coverage.

AUTO INSURANCE POLICY COMPARISON SHEET

Insurance company _____

liability
 single limit
 split limits
 bodily injury limits
 property damage limits
 premium
medical payments
 coverage limits
 premium
uninsured motorist
 coverage limits
 premium

TIPS FOR SHOPPING FOR CAR INSURANCE

AUTO INSURANCE POLICY COMPARISON SHEET				
Insurance company				
underinsured motorist				
coverage limits				
premium				
collision				
coverage limits				
deductible				
premium				
other than collision				
coverage limits				
deductible				
premium				
towing and labor				
coverage limits				
premium				

AUTO INSURANCE POLICY COMPARISON SHEET

Insurance company _____

rental reimbursement
   coverage limits
   premium
other coverages
   coverage limits
   premium
total premium
Does the company use specific repair centers?

TIPS FOR SHOPPING FOR CAR INSURANCE

AUTO INSURANCE POLICY COMPARISON SHEET			
Insurance company			
What other cost-containment tools does it use?			
Does the company ever pay dividends or other rebates?			
Where is the closest adjuster or accident center?			
How does the state insurance department rate this company? (Or has it received many complaints?)			

Armed with your chart, you're ready to start shopping.

Once you've got a list of prices and company rate comparisons, you can start looking at ways to reduce standard premiums. These include:

- Drop the **rental-reimbursement** coverage. Rental coverage pays for renting a car when your own auto is in the repair shop. If you have two cars, you might be able to get along without a rental.

- Drop **towing and labor costs** coverage. If you already have coverage—through an automobile club, for example—you're just duplicating your costs.

- Drop **loss of income** benefits. You may want to skip this coverage if you have a good disability plan at work.

- Cancel coverage if your car won't be used for a long period. If you're flying out of the country on vacation for **a month or longer**, see if you can cancel your coverage for collision while you're gone.

- Don't forget to ask about special discounts. Many companies offer price breaks to people who drive **fewer miles** than the annual average. Most also offer lower rates to motorists who haven't had an accident or moving violation for three years. And the traditional **good student discount** can save as much as 25 percent of premiums—if you have teenage or young-adult drivers in your household (more on this later).

- Ask about **safety-feature discounts**: There may be a break if you have air bags, anti-lock brakes, alarm or anti-theft systems.

- If you have two cars, you may be able to cut your costs by insuring them both with the same company rather than looking for different insurers for each. Discounts for **multiple-car households** can range up to 15 percent.

- Consider joining a car pool or take public transit to work. Insurers base your premiums in part on how much time you're driving.

- Check out insurance costs when considering a move. Insurance companies base their rates partly on **where you live**. People living in big cities probably will pay more than those in small towns, all other things being equal. Rates can even vary from one block or ZIP code to another because of lower accident or theft rates.

- Buy cars with better insurance records. Generally, expensive cars cost more to insure than budget boxes; sports cars carry heftier premiums than family sedans. Cars that are more **popular targets of thieves** also can cost more to insure.

- Insure your house with the same company. So-called **multi-policy discounts** shave a few percentage points off your homeowners' and auto insurance policies.

CHAPTER 9

FAMILY RISKS AND RATES

The insurance consumers with the best incentive for shopping premiums and coverage are people who have families with several drivers. (This gets back to the recurring issue of **households** and insurance.) Multiple driver policies get very expensive for one main reason: **teenagers**. They cause more accidents per capita than any other demographic group.

> Two related demographic notes. First, gender doesn't make as big a difference in the accident rates of teenage drivers as you might think. Girls are almost as dangerous as boys on this count. Second, while young drivers are the most dangerous group per capita, drivers over 65 are the most dangerous drivers per mile driven. The difference is that people over 65 drive fewer miles than teenagers.

Here are some effective ways to save money on **family auto insurance**:

- It's usually best to stay with the company you've done business with for several years—the longer you're a good customer, the better rates they usually offer.

- Most major insurance carriers reduce premiums for drivers up to age 21 by 10 to 15 percent if they take a certified driver education course. Make sure your kids take driver's ed. If their school has no program, a course at a certified privately run driving school will also qualify you for the discount.

- Most insurance companies provide a discount for students with a B average or better or a 3.0 grade point average in college. The typical discount is 10 percent. Some insurance companies ask for copies of report cards or transcripts each time you renew your policy.

- If a student leaves home to go to school more than 100 miles away, the parents can get a policy discount because the teen driver is not around as much to drive.

- Intermediate size cars, sedans and other "low profile" vehicles will carry lower premiums than high-performance cars, sport utility vehicles and sports cars. If a teenager wants to drive a sports car, you have to go to a company specializing in high-risk policies. The premium can be double the normal rates.

- It is usually cheaper to put a teenage driver on the parents' policy than it is to buy him separate insurance. Even if the teenager has his own car, including his coverage on the family policy might help get the multi-car discount—most companies offer 10 to 30 percent.

- However, if a teenager has his own car and doesn't qualify for a good student or driver education discount, it may be better for him to have his own policy—especially if he has a bad driving record.

- You can cut the cost of policy premiums by raising the deductible amounts or dropping collision, fire and theft coverage for the cars the teenager drives. Many agents suggest a deductible of $500 for collision, $250 for theft and other damage and dropping towing and labor coverage. This approach is especially applicable if you give a kid an older car.

- If a teenage driver is in an accident which is not judged another driver's fault or gets a traffic ticket, the cost of your policy will rise, often dramatically.

DEDUCTIBLES

Another point to consider when you're comparing policies: What kind of **deductibles** to include in your insurance package. To play it safe, assume that if you choose a deductible you'll have to pay it once a year. This assumption budgets in the deductible as a cost of coverage.

One of the major factors affecting the price of collision coverage is the deductible. And this is something that you can control.

A deductible is simply a risk that is **self-insured**. With a $1,000 deductible, the driver self-insures the first $1,000 of each loss. So a driver needs to ask how frequent such losses might be, how many autos are being insured and how many loss-free years you will need to drive before the premium savings equal the **extra risk** being taken.

TIPS FOR SHOPPING FOR CAR INSURANCE

> If all other factors are equal, the greater the deductible amount, the lower the cost for collision insurance. This is true because higher deductibles reduce the insurance company's exposure. Small losses which do not exceed the deductible do not require a claim settlement, and large losses which exceed the deductible result in a smaller settlement.

Deductibles usually range from $100 to $500 per claim. Other deductibles, ranging from as low as $50 to as high as $1,000, are commonly available for collision coverage. A caveat: If you finance your car, the finance company may not let you have a high deductible.

> To determine whether a deductible works for you, compare a year's premiums without to a year's premiums with a deductible plus that deductible. The deductible total will be higher. But, if you go through the year without making a claim, you get to keep the deductible amount.

In most cases, insurance companies will structure premiums to **encourage high deductibles**. For example, the cost of collision coverage with a $500 deductible can be as much as 45 percent less than the cost with a $100 deductible. In this scenario, a $500 deductible will pay for itself in premium savings in as little as three years. A $1,000 deductible can pay for itself in just a little longer than that. But both of these scenarios assume you don't make any claims during that period.

DEDUCTIBLE/PREMIUM GRID				
Insurance company:	premium	premium	premium	premium
personal injury				
$0				
$100				
$250				
$500				
$1000				
collision				
$0				
$100				
$250				
$500				
$1000				

TIPS FOR SHOPPING FOR CAR INSURANCE

DEDUCTIBLE/PREMIUM GRID

Insurance company:

	premium	premium	premium	premium
other than collision				
$0				
$100				
$250				
$500				
$1000				
other coverage				
$0				
$100				
$250				
$500				
$1000				

The intent of deductibles is to encourage drivers to **assume responsibility** for the smaller, more affordable losses that can occur to a car. (They don't usually apply to liability or medical payment claims.) This eliminates small claims and paperwork for the insurance company and helps keep premiums down.

If the damage to your car is smaller than your deductible or even close to your deductible amount (between $500 and $1000 in most cases—though the amount varies), it might make the most sense **not to make a claim** at all. You can shop around, pay cash for the repair and never tell your insurance company. This prevents the company from noting that you had the accident.

> In situations where you're the at-fault driver and have a deductible for liability claims, you can offer to pay for the repairs to the other person's car yourself.

Some people will want to pay for damages **out of pocket**, even if they have no deductible. The presence of an at-fault accident in someone's claims history (especially **if it's not the first**) can raise premiums dramatically enough that it's worth avoiding the claim all together.

DIRECT MARKETING

Increasingly, smart consumers are buying their auto insurance **directly from insurance companies.** You can do this through the mail, on the telephone, or—the most recent development—via on-line computer services.

The on-line services are an area in which most insurance companies see marketing potential. They predict a day when you can tap into a computer and see a comparative list of auto insurance rates offered by each company.

Armed with this information, you could set the agenda when it comes time to bargain for the policy that will cover that prized car, trusty family wagon, or at least keep you on the road legally.

This will require a greater level of consumer sophistication. You'll need to know more about what coverages you need and what your buying with your premium dollars.

Here's a list of suggestions for trimming auto insurance charges when you're dealing directly with an insurance company:

- Cancel **collision** coverage on older cars. On cars that are financed, banks require collision, which pays for damage to a driver's own car when he or she is involved in a wreck, and comprehensive, which pays for theft, fire and other losses. But once the loans are paid off and the cars get five or six years old, a driver may want to drop one or both coverages.
- Weigh the cost of comprehensive and collision coverage against the value of the

car. Anytime that **values gets below $3,000**, it's a good time to look at the coverage.

- The same basic rule applies with **comprehensive** insurance, which covers a grab-bag of things—vandalism, theft, explosion, hitting an animal, fire, etc.

- If your state's laws allow it, drop your auto **medical payments** coverage. Medical payments coverages take care of medical bills for you and your family, regardless of who is at fault in an accident. If you and your family already have good health insurance, you probably don't need medical coverage through your auto policy.

- Try to avoid getting tickets. The more traffic violations a driver has, the more recoupment charges he or she must pay. A driver with more than five experience points on his or her record can pay double—and sometimes even triple—standard premiums.

- Cut the costs of **teenagers**. Teenagers who have driver's licenses are expensive to insure. In fact, adding a teenager to a two-driver, two-car policy can boost a family's premiums by 50 percent. To cut your costs, see if the insurer offers discounts for students who have taken a driver's education course or have good grades.

- Get a discount when your child goes to college. Many insurers will reduce your premiums when your child is at college, so long as the school is at least 100 miles away from your home.

- If you're a senior citizen, check out **driver safety course** discounts. Some companies offer 10 percent or more off their standard policies for drivers who are age 50 or older. (However, those discounts may not apply to drivers who are older than 65, for example.)

- Let your insurance company know if you keep your car in a **garage**. Cars in garages are less likely to be hit in the middle of the night by errant drivers than cars left on the street. Garaged cars also are less likely to be stolen.

- Find out whether an agent can get you a better deal. After you've done your own shopping and comparing, you can go to an **independent insurance agent**—someone who sells policies from several companies for a commission—and see if he or she can find a lower price.

- **Look ahead:** What happens if you get in an accident? What if you're in two accidents in a year? It's worth knowing how accidents and claims might affect your future rates. And how the insurance company you choose handles claims.

- Don't smoke. Several companies offer lower rates to nonsmokers than smokers. Reason: Smoking is thought of as a higher-risk behavior.

CHAPTER 9

Finally, to prepare for the logical end of the shopping process, review a standard auto insurance application form. You'll find all of the elements of coverage we've considered addressed in it.

TIPS FOR SHOPPING FOR CAR INSURANCE

COVERAGES/PREMIUMS

COVERAGE		LIMITS OF LIABILITY						VEHICLE 1	VEHICLE 2	VEHICLE 3	VEHICLE 4
SINGLE LIMIT LIABILITY	$	EACH ACCIDENT						$	$	$	$
BODILY INJURY	$	EACH PERSON $				EACH ACCIDENT		$	$	$	$
PROPERTY DAMAGE	$	EACH ACCIDENT						$	$	$	$
PERSONAL INJ. PROTECTION	$		$			DEDUCTIBLE		$	$	$	$
MEDICAL PAYMENTS	$	EACH PERSON						$	$	$	$
UNINSURED MOTORIST CSL/B.I. / P.D.	$ / $	EACH PERSON $ / EACH ACCIDENT				EACH ACCIDENT		$	$	$	$
UNDERINSURED MOTORIST CSL/B.I. / P.D.	$ / $	EACH PERSON $ / EACH ACCIDENT				EACH ACCIDENT		$	$	$	$
COMPREHENSIVE	DED. 1 $	2 $	3 $	4 $		ACV UNLESS AMT. STATED		$	$	$	$
COLLISION	DED. 1 $	2 $	3 $	4 $				$	$	$	$
TOWING & LABOR	1 $	2 $	3 $	4 $				$	$	$	$
RENTAL REIMBURSEMENT	1 $	2 $	3 $	4 $				$	$	$	$
ADDITIONAL COVERAGES/ENDORSEMENTS								$	$	$	$
							TOTAL PER VEHICLE	$	$	$	$

ESTIMATED TOTAL	DEPOSIT	BALANCE DUE
$	$	$

168

CHAPTER 9

CONCLUSION

Just about every consumer advocate tells you to shop around and compare prices and products before you buy something as expensive as auto insurance. The problem is that shopping for insurance can be complicated.

The best way to think of shopping for insurance is that there are two issues occurring at once: The premiums that different insurance companies will charge for the same kind of coverage and the premiums that each individual company will charge for variations on the standard insurance package.

Most insurance professionals suggest that you start by comparing the prices and levels of service among different companies. Once you've selected one or two that work best for you, adjust items like deductibles and coverage limits until you have a package that suits your needs—and that you can afford.

CHAPTER 10

HOW INSURANCE COMPANIES PRICE COVERAGE

Within the insurance industry, professionals refer to pricing insurance coverage as **rating**. A rate is the cost for a unit of insurance. As you might guess, some methods had to be devised for charging individual policyholders appropriate prices for different amounts of coverage.

As a smart consumer, you should have a basic understanding of these methods—so you know how insurance companies look at you and your car when they calculate what you have to pay for coverage.

With automobile insurance, a **base rate** is published for each specific kind of coverage, such as bodily injury and property damage liability. For example, a base rate might be $300 for $100,000 of liability coverage. A driver with a good driving record might qualify for this base rate, while a driver with a poor driving record must be charged an increased amount to reflect the poor record. This increased amount is computed by multiplying the base rate by a **rating factor**.

HOW INSURANCE COMPANIES PRICE COVERAGE

Rating is an important function in the insurance industry. In order for insurance companies to be financially stable, rates must be adequate to cover costs. In order for insurance companies to remain competitive, rates must be fair and reasonable in **relation to the risk** of loss.

> Insurance companies and rating bureaus use a broad statistical base of loss and expense experience when developing rates.

Increasingly, though, states don't allow insurance companies to share **pricing information**. As a result, different companies may quote the same driver wildly divergent prices. This is because some companies consider certain characteristics—such as your age or your driving record—as more of a risk than other companies do.

There's not even much agreement in the industry about the philosophy behind pricing insurance. Some people think premiums should be **higher than market averages.**

In a 1994 report to the insurance practice section of the American Bar Association, University of Florida law professor Richard Pearson wrote that reduced auto insurance costs may not be in the public's best interest. "From an economic perspective," he argued, "lowering the cost of driving is not necessarily socially desirable."

> Pearson concluded that *artificially low* insurance premiums understate the true cost of accidents, which includes pain and suffering damages, and lead to more driving by people who can't afford insurance. This leads to more accidents that the insured drivers have to cover.

HOW RATING INFORMATION IS SHARED

In order to have consistent rating information without colluding, most insurance companies use rating manuals based on a standard manual published by the Insurance Services Office—an industry trade group. The ISO's standard manual suggests rating rules. Among the most important are:

- **Defined Autos and Eligibility**

    Generally, *private passenger autos* are four wheel vehicles, such as sedans and station wagons, which are not used to carry passengers for a fee and are not rented to others. *Pickups and vans* are treated as private passenger autos if they do not exceed weight limits, and are not used in a delivery or freight business (except farming operations which are permitted).

- Ownership

    Under the general eligibility rules, a private passenger auto must be owned or leased by an individual or married couple who live together. However, a Personal

Auto Policy may also be issued to cover an auto owned by relatives other than husband and wife, or an auto owned by unrelated individuals who reside together, if a Joint Ownership endorsement is attached to the policy.

- **Automobile Classifications**

    Several types of classifications are considered in the rating of automobile risks. Some relate to the use of covered autos, some relate to the operators of the autos, and some relate to the automobiles.

- **Policy Period**

    This is, simply, the amount of time for which a policy is in force.

Rates and premiums for physical damage coverage are based on the **value of covered cars**. Generally, the maximum exposure for the insurance company is a known amount. For this reason, unlike the other coverages we have studied, a limit of liability is not shown in the Declarations for physical damage, and is not usually necessary. Instead, we find provisions which impose limitations on the amount that will be paid for any loss.

> To calculate rates, most insurance companies use rating charts or tables that include the various relevant factors. An agent, broker or salesperson uses these charts to find a premium dollar amount.

CHAPTER 10

RATES AND PREMIUMS

Automobile rating determines base rates and applicable rating factors, and then calculates **individual coverage premiums** and the **total premium** for the policy.

A premium is the product of the base rate multiplied by the applicable rating factor. Separate premiums are determined for each of the **four major personal auto coverages**—liability, medical payments, collision and other than collision. These separate premiums are then added together to obtain the total policy premium.

THIS IS A SAMPLE OF INDIVIDUAL PREMIUMS FOR A STANDARD AUTOMOBILE INSURANCE POLICY.

Coverage	Base Premium	x	Total Factor	=	Premium
BI/PD Liability	170	x	1.00	=	$170
Med Pay	12	x	1.00	=	$ 12
UM				=	$ 18
Comprehensive	74	x	1.00	=	$ 74
Collision	93	x	1.00	=	$ 93

In this example, we have used a total factor of 1.00. Depending on the factors relevant to a given policyholder and a given car, this number can change.

Traditional auto insurance rates are based on broad averages of **loss and expense data** and include components for expected losses and expenses. Individual companies have generally been permitted to deviate from published rates based on individual company differences in experience and expense factors.

In recent years, the insurance industry has begun a transition toward some new rating approaches. The Insurance Services Offices has begun to develop **prospective loss costs** for a number of lines of insurance, including automobile insurance. Prospective loss costs are based on loss data and loss adjustment expenses, but not the other components of a final rate (such as an insurance company's expenses and profit).

Insurers that use prospective loss costs must apply modifications in the form of a **loss cost multiplier** to account for individual company expenses, underwriting profit and contingencies, in order to arrive at final rates. Generally, individual companies believe loss cost rating gives them more flexibility in developing their rates.

PRIMARY AND SECONDARY RATING FACTORS

To take into consideration the differences between different automobile risks, the insurance industry uses a system of **primary and secondary rating factors**, which are added together to produce a **total rating factor**.

CHAPTER 10

> The primary rating factor is based upon many things, including use of the vehicle and the age and sex of the drivers. For youthful operators, the primary factor is also affected by marital status, driver training, and scholastic achievement. We considered these factors in the previous chapter.

The total rating factor is then multiplied by the base rate for all major coverages—except uninsured motorists coverage. Rating factors do not apply to UM coverage, or to towing or other **minor coverages** that may be added by endorsement.

In most states, **territorial rating** of automobile risks is permitted and insurance companies do consider the neighborhood in which you live. This means the primary rating factor also depends on the territory where the vehicle is garaged (this means where it is parked at night, even if it is parked on the street). Usually, this location is the same as the address of a policy's **named insured**.

Different areas pay different rates because of a number of factors: state insurance requirements, local population, weather conditions, collision damage repair costs, auto theft rates and hospital costs.

Also, insurance companies charge customers in a particular area for the cost of nearby accidents involving uninsured drivers.

Premium ranges vary from state to state. In 1995, drivers in Hawaii paid the highest premiums in the country, an average of nearly $1000 a year; drivers in North Dakota paid the lowest, an average of less than $350 a year.

Other than the state you live and drive in, a consistent set of factors determine the premiums you pay for auto insurance. These include:

- who you are;
- your driving record;
- where you live—within the state;
- how you use your car;
- the model, mileage and year of your car; and
- the type of coverage you select.

THE DRIVER'S AGE

Perhaps the most hotly disputed rating factor is **age**. As with most insurance coverage, it is illegal to discriminate against a person because of age in the **issuance, nonrenewal,** or **cancellation** of an automobile insurance policy. What insurance companies can do is structure premiums to accomplish their goals.

For most men and women, auto premiums actually drop a bit while they're in their 50s. The rate of **accidents per miles driven** is lower for people in the 40s and 50s than any other group. Insurance companies know this and respond accordingly.

CHAPTER 10

> Since older people tend to drive less and to avoid the most dangerous conditions (at night, during rush hour and in bad weather) fewer older people than teenagers die on the roads. That means older people tend to pay lower insurance rates than even middle-aged drivers.

Accident rates—and premiums—begin creeping up again when drivers reach 60; over age 75, the rate of fatal crashes per miles driven is even higher than it is for teenagers.

The accident numbers for the oldest drivers skew perceptions among auto insurance risk analysts. They tend to characterize the entire population of over-65 drivers as **high risk**. This means that drivers between 65 and 75, whose accident rates remain relatively close to drivers in the middle-age categories, subsidize the drivers over 75.

"A logical step would be to adjust premiums so that the oldest drivers paid much higher rates," says one risk analyst for a big multiline insurance company. He requested anonymity for his comments on this subject. "But that would effectively force people over 70—certainly over 75—off the roads. The political fall-out from that would be huge. There wouldn't be an elected official in Florida who still had a job."

The American Association of Retired Persons and other groups offer driver **safety training** courses for people over 50. The AARP stresses that the entire group—its target market—has more accidents per mile driven than any other age group. But some insurance industry professionals argue this is merely an attempt to spread risk.

Proposed plans for reducing older drivers' accident rates include **tighter relicensing rules** to ensure that their vision or other capabilities haven't fallen below minimum levels.

> In 1994, sixteen states had age-based license renewal regulations, but advocacy groups like the AARP considers them discriminatory. "As a general rule," said Ted Bobrow, an AARP auto insurance specialist, "we oppose age-based testing. It may be a good idea to test all drivers every year or every four years."

RATING THE CAR

Collision coverage pays you for loss or damage to your own automobile as the result of upset, overturn or collision with another object. In order to provide this kind of insurance, a company has to calculate how much your car is worth and then calculate how much it will charge in premiums. To avoid inconsistencies, the insurance industry uses standard formulas for calculating premiums.

Four factors influence auto insurance premiums:

- the age of the vehicle,

CHAPTER 10

- the value of the vehicle,
- the deductible amount you've chosen, and
- the territory in which the vehicle is located.

If all other factors are equal, the older the vehicle the less the cost for collision coverage. Most vehicles wear out with use and the replacement value declines over time.

Shown below is a section of a sample **rate table** used by insurance companies to calculate the risk factors that influence the insured value of a car. The base rate for collision coverage for a particular automobile is where the appropriate territory, age group, and symbol columns intersect.

Auto No	Classification Code	Primary Factor	+	Secondary Factor	=	Total Factor
1	_____	_____	+	_____	=	_____

Symbol _____   Age Group _____   Terr. _____

HOW INSURANCE COMPANIES PRICE COVERAGE

Auto 1				
Coverage	Base Rate	× Total Factor	=	Premium
$ _____ BI	_____	× _____	=	_____
$ _____ PD	_____	× _____	=	_____
$ _____ BI/PD SL	_____	× _____	=	_____
$ _____ MP	_____	× _____	=	_____
$ _____ UM			=	_____
$ _____ Ded. COMP	_____	× _____	=	_____
$ _____ Ded. COLL	_____	× _____	=	_____
$ _____ TOWING				_____
			TOTAL	$ _____

The higher the **age group** number, the lower the rate. This suggests that older vehicles are assigned to a higher age group, which is true.

A convenient way to figure the age group of an automobile: First determine the **current model year**. If it is prior to October 1, the current calendar year is the current model year. If the date is October 1 or later in the year, the next calendar year is considered the current model year. Thus, if the current date is November 1, 1994, you call it 1995.

> Once you have determined the current model year, you simply count backwards. If 1995 is the current model year, the next earlier year would be 1994, preceded by 1993, etc. Since age group 6 is the maximum age, all automobiles which are 1990 or earlier models would—in 1995—fall into age group 6.

Some insurance companies use rate tables that show **vehicle model years** instead of age groups. The rating concept is the same whether you are using actual model years or age groups.

The second factor which affects collision rates is the value of the vehicle, which is reflected by the **symbol group**. The symbol group is a rating code developed by adjusting an automobile's **price new** upward or downward to reflect the physical damage loss experience for that particular model.

Two automobiles of different makes and models might have the same market value, but be assigned to different symbol groups if one tends to suffer **greater damage** in an equal crash, or if it is **more expensive** to repair equal damage in one model because of the cost of individual parts.

> You can think of the symbol group as something that reflects the value of a vehicle and the insurance company's relative exposure to loss.

The higher the symbol group code, the higher the rate. The key to identifying an automobile is the **vehicle identification number** or VIN. Although an actual VIN may consist of 17 characters, only the first eight are critical to the rating process.

> The rating symbol group code is based on the first eight characters of an automobile's VIN.

This information is also useful to insurance companies in various ways. For example, if an application states that an auto is a two-door model with a small engine and the VIN indicates that it is a four-door with a big engine, the company will likely double-check to determine which description is correct.

The additional characters in a VIN are useful for confirming the identity of a specific automobile. While they do not affect rating, they indicate the specific **manufacturing or assembly plant** and even the **production unit number** of each completed vehicle that comes off the production line. Each automobile VIN is unique in this respect. Thus, when a **stolen vehicle** is recovered, the police may use the VIN to confirm that an automobile belongs to a specific registered owner.

RATING FOR COMPREHENSIVE COVERAGE

Other than collision or **comprehensive** insurance is a physical damage coverage that applies to your own vehicle for losses other than those caused by collision.

All of the procedures you just used to determine collision rates also apply to determining the comprehensive rate. Comprehensive coverage is usually rated by **territory, age group, symbol group,** and **deductible amount.**

> Alternative comprehensive deductibles, ranging from $50 to $1,000, are usually available. In some states, full coverage may be written with no deductible.

Most rating tables include different secondary factors for standard, intermediate and high performance vehicles, and for sports vehicles. Among the **four most common performance codes:**

- "i" means intermediate,
- "h" means high performance,
- "s" means sports model, and
- "p" means sports premium model.

If a car model doesn't have a specific performance code, it is presumed to be a standard performance model. Most cars are **standard** performance vehicles.

RATING THE DRIVER

The most important classification that affects the secondary rating factor is the **sub-class,** which is based on the driving record of the policyholder or other drivers living in the same household. The applicable subclass for an automobile is based on a series of **points** (from 0 to 4) which may be assigned because of **motor vehicle violations or accidents.**

> These points are different than points that your state's department of motor vehicles or public safety may charge against your driver's license to track violations.

Many companies assign points based on the **Safe Driver Insurance Plan** which is part of the standard rating manual published by the Insurance Services Office. This Plan lists types of violations or accidents and assigns a point value based on the **severity** of the problem.

> Example: While initially rating your auto policy, your insurance company discovers that a point should be charged for an accident. This point increases your secondary rating factor from 0.00 to 0.40 and the total factor from 1.30 to 1.70. The base premium affected was $400. Therefore, instead of paying $520, you will pay $680.

Every accident does not result in points being charged. But points (or, usually, one point) are assigned for cer-

CHAPTER 10

tain **inexperienced drivers**, even if they've had no accidents or convictions.

The chart below shows how points are assigned and adjusted in the case of households that include **youthful operator** and seek a **good student** discount.

PRIMARY CLASSIFICATIONS
RATING FACTORS AND STATISTICAL CODES

YOUTHFUL OPERATOR
GOOD STUDENT CLASSIFICATIONS

AGE			UNMARRIED MALE	
			Not Owner or Principal Operator	
			Pleasure Use or Farm Use	Drive to Work or Business Use
WITHOUT DRIVER TRAINING	17 or Less	Factor Code	2.05 8514--	2.30 8515--
	18	Factor Code	1.90 8524--	2.15 8525--
	19	Factor Code	1.80 8534--	2.05 8535--
	20	Factor Code	1.65 8544--	1.90 8545--
WITH DRIVER TRAINING	17 or Less	Factor Code	1.75 8564--	2.00 8565
	18	Factor Code	1.60 8574--	1.85 8575--
	19	Factor Code	1.50 8584--	1.75 8585--
	20	Factor Code	1.35 8594--	1.60 8595--
WITH OR WITHOUT DRIVER TRAINING	21 thru 24	Factor Code	1.20 8614--	1.45 8615--

	AGE		UNMARRIED MALE	
			Owner or Principal Operator	
			Pleasure Use or Farm Use	Drive to Work or Business Use
WITHOUT DRIVER TRAINING	17 or Less	Factor Code	2.70 8724--	2.95 8715--
	18	Factor Code	2.50 8724--	2.75 8725--
	19	Factor Code	2.30 8734--	2.55 8735--
	20	Factor Code	2.10 8744--	2.35 8745--
WITH DRIVER TRAINING	17 or Less	Factor Code	2.50 8574--	2.75 8765
	18	Factor Code	2.30 8774--	2.55 8775--
	19	Factor Code	2.15 8784--	2.40 8785--
	20	Factor Code	2.05 8794--	2.30 8795--
WITH OR WITHOUT DRIVER TRAINING	21 thru 24	Factor Code	1.45 8814--	2.25 8815--

The rates would be even higher if the young driver didn't qualify for a good student discount.

Three conditions are necessary in order for points to apply on the basis of an inexperienced operator: The person must be licensed less than three years, be the principal operator of the auto, and have no points charged due to an accident.

Auto insurance **reform measures** have focused on driving records and experience as the most secondary factors. For example, California's Proposition 103 gave rating priority to a driver's record, the number of miles driven per year and the number of years of driving experience over all other factors in setting rates.

> Other—more recent—reforms have attempted to reverse that trend. They allow insurers to attach no more weight to drivers' records than other factors, such as their residential ZIP codes, marital status and gender.

While some reform laws lay out the order of factors to be considered, many do not provide priority weights for each. This is a major technical criticism of populist reforms. The absence of priority weights allows insurance companies to use **sequential analysis**. This leaves rating priorities to the company's discretion and—argue most analysts—raises the prospect of rates based on where you live rather than how you drive.

RATING FAMILY POLICIES

The manner in which rating factors are applied to multi-car policies sounds complicated—but is actually pretty simple. There are **two key elements** to remember:

- When rating more than one car, driving record points are applied to a maximum of two cars. When rating three or more cars, the driving record points are assigned to the two cars with the highest base premium. All additional cars don't have to have points.

- When there are no youthful operators, the primary factor for the principal operator of a car is applied to that car. If you add youthful operators to your policy, the primary factors for youthful operators will apply to all vehicles those drivers use.

In all cases, if any youthful operator is the **principal operator** of a car, the primary factor for that young driver applies to that car.

Although youthful operators who are not principal operators are assigned to cars in the order of the cars having the highest **base premiums**, it is possible for two or more cars to have the same base premium. There is a rating rule to resolve this potential conflict when it arises.

If the total base premium is the same for two or more cars, a youthful operator who is not a principal operator will be assigned to the car with the lowest rated **use classification** (the "pleasure" versus "business" distinction).

CONCLUSION

Rating is the process insurance companies use to calculate how much to charge different people for the amount and kind of insurance they need. You don't have to be a rating expert in order to buy insurance smartly—but understanding how insurance companies use the information you give them can help you make better decisions when you fill out a policy application.

HOW INSURANCE COMPANIES PRICE COVERAGE

CHAPTER 11

HOW TO MAKE AN INSURANCE CLAIM

All the work you put into choosing the right kind of auto insurance comes to a point when you **make a claim** on your policy. Stirred by the emotions that often follow an accident, some people unleash anger and frustration at the adjusters and clerks who are part of the claims process.

It's important to remember that this is a **process**. Making a claim on your auto policy is like any other aspect of a contract transaction. The best companies will be supportive and understanding of what you've experienced. But what you really want is to have your claim paid.

In this chapter, we'll consider how you can make a claim in the most effective way. Throughout, a fairly consistent pattern emerges. In states that have passed insurance reforms aimed at limiting premiums, systematic problems related to claims making sometimes follow.

> It seems to be a market-driven response: If you pay less for insurance, you're likely to have more trouble making a claim.

MAKING THE CLAIM

When you do have to make a claim, don't be afraid to count on your **agent**—if you have one. Agents who are eager to keep your business will become your best advocates.

On the other hand, if they're not helpful or even difficult, don't hesitate to go to your **insurance company's consumer complaint department**. The fact that agents sometimes—and it's usually just sometimes—get in the way of making a claim is a big reason that a growing number of people deal directly with insurance companies.

If you don't know whom to call when you've been in an accident or your car has been stolen, look at your policy, billing statements or proof-of-insurance cards.

> Your correspondence with an insurance company will usually include a telephone number for making claims. These numbers are usually working 24 hours a day.

You can call the company from an accident scene—but people usually only do this when their car has been so badly damaged that it has to be towed away. If your car still runs, concentrate on getting the names, drivers' license numbers and vehicle ID information of everyone else involved.

> Each state has some form of financial responsibility or compulsory insurance law requiring automobile drivers to show that they are capable of paying accident claims against them up to a specified minimum amount. Generally, these laws require drivers to show proof of financial responsibility after they have been involved in an accident.

"Once something happens, you need to let us know immediately, because we may need to investigate something, like tire tracks for example, which don't stay around very long," says one spokeswoman for State Farm Insurance Companies. "Know who you were in an accident with. Get the other party's **insurance information**, the number on the **police report** and the **name of the person** who's insured before calling us."

> Although state laws vary on requiring drivers to make claims within a certain time period, most companies prefer that claims be filed within 15 days. If someone's been hurt in an accident, there's been serious damage or some law has been broken, call the police first. You can call your insurance company later.

Of course, insurance companies want to be **notified as quickly as possible**. And it's true that, the sooner you file a claim, the sooner you'll get a settlement.

The biggest reason you will probably have to call your insurance company quickly is to start coverage for **towing or a replacement rental car**—if you've chosen those optional coverages.

> Most states do require that insurance companies either process a claim, or at least tell you why it hasn't been processed, within either 60 or 90 days.

DUTIES AFTER AN ACCIDENT OR LOSS

A pretty good guide for how to make a claim exists right in your auto insurance policy. The standard policy includes a section called *Duties after a Loss*. This section specifies **what a person must do** in order to get recovery for losses covered by the policy.

The instructions are pretty straightforward:

> We have no duty to provide coverage under this policy unless there has been full compliance with the following duties:
>
> A. We must be notified promptly of how, when and where the accident or loss happened. Notice should also include the names and addresses of any injured persons and of any witnesses.

You should report a loss to the company as promptly as possible in order to give the insurance company the opportunity to act quickly to **settle the claim**. Generally, the longer a claim goes without settlement, the more it will cost. Prompt forwarding of legal papers and notices is extremely important since often they require a response or appearance within a limited time and, if not forwarded promptly, may result in **forfeitures or penalties**. Prompt notice of a hit and run or a stolen vehicle should be given to the police.

B. A person seeking any coverage must:

1. Cooperate with us in the investigation, settlement or defense of any claim or suit.

2. Promptly send us copies of any notices or legal papers received in connection with the accident or loss.

3. Submit, as often as we reasonably require:

a. to physical exams by physicians we select. We will pay for these exams.

b. to examination under oath and subscribe the same.

4. Authorize us to obtain:

a. medical reports; and

b. other pertinent records.

5. Submit a proof of loss when required by us.

C. A person seeking Uninsured Motorists Coverage must also:

1. Promptly notify the police if a hit-and-run driver is involved.

2. Promptly send us copies of the legal papers if a suit is brought.

D. A person seeking Coverage for Damage to Your Auto must also:

1. Take reasonable steps after loss to protect "your covered auto" or any "non-owned auto" and their equipment from further loss. We will pay reasonable expenses incurred to do this.

2. Promptly notify the policy if "your covered auto" or any "non-owned auto" is stolen.

3. Permit us to inspect and appraise the damaged property before its repair or disposal.

The five duties listed under part B apply to any person seeking coverage under **any part of the policy**. The duties listed under part C apply only when a claim is being submitted for coverage under **uninsured motorists coverage**.

> If these duties are not carried out, the insurance company is not obligated to pay a loss.

MORE THAN JUST THE MECHANICS

The mechanics of contacting your insurance company and the police after you've suffered a loss are relatively simple. But you want to more than just comply with the rules when you make a claim—you want to do it

CHAPTER 11

in a way that assures you the maximum timely settlement.

In order to do this, you need to remember how the insurance company looks at a claim.

> Insurance companies use the term limit of liability because when a loss occurs which is covered by the policy, they become legally responsible for honoring their contractual agreement to pay damages to you or to a third party on your behalf. The liability—and the limits—applies to the insurance company.

The limit of liability for any coverage is simply the amount of coverage, the **maximum amount of insurance** or upper limit that the insurance company is legally obligated to pay if a covered loss occurs. If a covered loss occurs for less than the limit of liability, the insurance company will pay the amount of the loss (minus any deductible that may apply). If the amount of a covered loss is more than the limit of liability, the insurance company will pay the limit of its coverage **and you are responsible for paying any additional costs.**

> If your insurance company sells you or renews for you any policy that does not satisfy the financial responsibility law of your state, that policy must come with a clear, written warning that it does not meet the law.

The limit of liability for physical damage coverage is not a specific amount—it's usually the **actual cash value** (ACV) minus any deductible.

ACV generally means **replacement cost minus depreciation**. Most cars depreciate in value over time. If you paid $10,000 for a new car five years ago and it is totally destroyed today, it would not be worth its original cost nor would it be worth the current cost for a new car. Instead, your insurance company would pay the ACV, and you might receive $3,500 as a settlement.

> Generally, the ACV should allow you to purchase another five-year-old car of the same (or similar) make and model.

If your car was not a total loss, the company will pay what it would cost to repair the car with materials of **like kind and quality** (which may mean using used or substitute parts).

DEFENSE COSTS

Because defending a suit in court can be very expensive, payment of **defense costs** is an important part of liability insurance coverage. In some cases, the cost of defense can be as much as, or more than, the amount ultimately awarded as damages.

> *Defend* means to resist the claim or go to court and try to show that the insured is not liable and should therefore not be required to pay the damages.

An **insuring agreement** in a standard policy consists of one or more statements made by the insurer, under which it makes contractual commitments which are binding as long as the insured pays the premium and complies with policy conditions. Automobile liability coverage applies to **bodily injury** (BI) and **property damage** (PD) for which you are legally liable. It also covers some miscellaneous related expenses.

The liability insuring agreement states that covered damages under the policy include prejudgment interest that a court may require a policyholder to pay. **Prejudgment interest** is interest on the amount of an award to an injured person, calculated from the time the injured person brings the suit to the time the court determined the damages. When a policyholder is required to pay such interest, it is covered as part of the liability damages the policy will pay, and the combined total of the damages and prejudgment interest is subject to the limit of liability.

The remainder of the insuring agreement states that, when a liability claim has been made against the insured, the insurance company has a choice of whether it will **settle (pay the damages) or defend.**

Defense costs are paid in addition to the policy liability limit, but the company's liability ends when it has paid out its liability limit. If you carry $100,000 of liability coverage, the company may pay the $100,000 to the injured party and owe no further obligation to you for defense. In addition, the company has no duty to defend a claim for injury or damage not covered by the policy.

> It's important to remember that the insurance company pays unlimited defense costs (in effect, there is no limit on defense costs) and that defense costs are paid in addition to the limit of liability.

If defense costs were included within the limit of liability, most of us would have to purchase much **higher limits of insurance** to be adequately protected. For example, if you had a $50,000 limit of liability and the insurer defended a claim for which your liability was questionable, but lost the case anyway and incurred $38,000 of expense for defense costs, there would only be $12,000 of coverage available for damages. If the damage award was $40,000, you would then have to pay $28,000 out of your own pocket.

The liability insuring agreement makes it clear that the insurance company is only obligated to defend claims which are, or may be, covered by the policy. It has no **duty to defend** or settle a claim for injury or damage which is not covered by the policy.

If the insurance company defends against a liability suit and the court reaches a verdict against you—and if the insurance company delays making the payment—the court might require that interest be paid on the amount of the judgment from the time it is entered until it is paid or an offer of payment is made. This interest is **post judgment interest**. It counts toward the policy's overall limit of liability.

In addition to payment of liability claims and costs of defending a suit, the company provides as additional amounts of coverage several supplementary payments:

- If you're involved in an accident involving bodily injury or property damage, the company will pay up to $250 toward the cost of a bail bond required because of the accident or a traffic violation arising out of the accident. However, the company is under no obligation to furnish the bond.

- The company will pay the cost, but not furnish any court bonds (such as appeal bonds or release of attachment bonds) for any suit the company defends.

However, if the insurance company should defend a suit, lose, and then decide to appeal, the insurance company would be responsible for the premium for any necessary appeal bond, and would pay for it under the supplementary payments section of the liability coverage.

The insurance company also agrees to pay for bonds to release *attachments* in any suit that it defends.

> For example: You have an accident in which you drive your car into the wall of someone else's garage. The garage owner has the right to attach your car (take it into custody) as a way of guaranteeing that you will pay for repairing the damage. If your insurance company decides to defend the suit against you rather than settle with the garage owner, under the supplementary payments coverage it will pay the premium for a bond to release the attachment of your car.

- The insuring agreement states that **prejudgment interest** is included, along with damages, in the limit of liability. But **postjudgment interest** is covered in addition to the limit of insurance under supplementary payments.
- Other expenses incurred at the company's request.

An interesting note: Most policies will pay up to $50 a day for **loss of earnings** (but not other income) you incur because of attendance at hearings and trials at the insurance company's request.

SUBROGATION AND INSURABLE INTEREST

To be **subrogated** means to be substituted in the place of another. In insurance policies, a subrogation provision says that if the insurance company has made a payment under the policy to you or to a third party on your behalf—and if you have a legal right to recover for that loss from another person—the insurance company is subrogated to your right.

> Subrogation is an important protection for the insurance company. It means it may seek recovery from a responsible third party.

Most automobile owners do not pay cash for their cars—instead, they borrow money from a bank or auto finance company to make the purchase. Until the loan is paid off, both the purchaser and the lender have a financial interest in the car, and this interest is said to be an **insurable interest**. Thus, virtually all banks or lending companies require that Damage to Your Auto coverage be carried on a financed vehicle and that they (as the lender) be listed on the policy as having an insurable interest in the car.

CALCULATING A SETTLEMENT

In most cases, there is **no dollar amount stated as a maximum limit** of coverage for collision or other than collision losses. The maximum limit is usually the actual cash value of the vehicle minus any deductible.

In determining what is the ACV for an entire vehicle or the damaged portion of one, an insurance company considers the amount of **depreciation** as a vehicle ages. Insurance adjusters also use tables that show **current market values** for different makes, models and years of vehicles, as well as standard values for repairs and replacement parts for the various vehicles.

The insurance company may either **repair or replace** a damaged vehicle, and it also has the option of simply paying the ACV of the stolen or damaged property. According to the standard policy provisions, the insurance company is only obligated to pay **the lesser of these amounts**.

In practice, the insurance company is likely to decide that the ACV is the lesser of the repair or replacement cost. When repair costs exceed the cost of replacing the entire vehicle, it will usually be considered a **total loss** and the settlement will be based on the current depreciated market value of the car. This same principle applies to total loss situations and to partial loss situations.

One key point to remember: Never accept a claim settlement that you believe is too low. If two repair shops say your damaged car needs to be fixed at a cost of $2,000, but the insurance company's adjuster offers you just $500, it's time to start **negotiating**.

> One good tactic: Ask the repair shop for line-item estimates that explain what needs to be done and why, and send these to all parties: your agent, the insurance company's director of consumer affairs, the manager of the claims department and anyone else involved.

If the insurance company still denies your claim or insists you take it to court for your money, **don't be intimidated**. Ask for the **language in your policy** or in state law that allows it to deny your claim. Save all paperwork and log all phone conversations with company representatives.

If what your insurance company says doesn't agree with your reading of your policy, ask your **state regulator** for help.

While state insurance commissioners usually have **no legal authority** to force an insurance company to pay an individual claim, the commissioner can fine a company or take other punitive actions if an insurer makes a **practice of unfairly underpaying** or denying claims.

DELAYING PAYMENT

Insurance companies used to settle claims more **quickly** than they do today. The theory was that if they settled quickly, they could do so for a smaller amount—they'd just make sure the policyholder signed a release denying any further claims related to the accident in question. But, as policies have become more complicated and releases harder to enforce, many insurance companies have changed their tactics.

> Now, many insurance companies delay payments as long as they can without inviting lawsuits.

You don't have to accept the delays, though. There are several **basic principles** that you should use in collecting from insurance companies:

- Analyze **every part of an accident** or other loss for how it might be covered by your policy—liability, collision, medical payments, uninsured motorists. Do this even if it means **waiting a day or two** to call your insurance company. (Rules change by state and specific policy, but you can usually wait as long as two weeks to report an accident to your insurance company.)

- Consider **all of the claims** you might make following an accident or loss. If you have health insurance, homeowners or renters, can you make claims under these coverages?

- Never accept a **first offer**—or even a first denial—by an insurance company as the final, unequivocal word. You know insurance companies will delay or deny claims if they can. If they do, ask for an explanation for their delay or denial. In response, you should **gather facts** and **reread your policies** yourself. If you can't decipher everything in the policy, talk to your agent or—if necessary—a lawyer.

Even if denial isn't an insurance company's ultimate goal, by playing the **denial game**, it can achieve something almost as advantageous—a lengthy delay in paying the claim. The longer an insurance company can hold on to its money, the better off it is.

CHAPTER 11

> But the law, and more importantly the courts, don't give insurance companies free rein to delay fair settlements as they please.

In the spring of 1995, the largest auto insurance carrier in Northern California had settled a massive lawsuit that charged the company with **refusing to pay the medical bills** of 78 accident victims.

The lawsuit had begun as 78 separate complaints, and the complaints were consolidated in 1991. Each policyholder had been insured by the California State Automobile Association in the late 1980s, and each told a similar story of being in a car wreck, getting treatment and having his or her benefits delayed—or denied—after an examination by a company doctor.

According to lawyers who worked on the case, CSAA decided in 1987 to stop paying for treatments by chiropractors and other doctors of soft-tissue injuries, the bruises and strains that often result from car accidents. But company officials denied making any such decision, contending that they were merely taking more time to investigate sudden increases in the number and expense of questionable claims.

But a criminal investigation had bolstered the policyholders' claims. In 1991, the San Francisco district attorney's office and the state Department of Insurance had opened investigations into allegations that CSAA was paying claims late, in part or not at all. The investigations ended a year later when the company agreed to pay about $260,000 in what it called assessments.

CSAA spokesman Barry Shiller said the cost of policyholders' medical claims had jumped 42 percent from 1985 through 1987, and that soft-tissue claims were the single biggest cause. "The [policyholders] did not think that it was reasonable to ask them to look at a health care bill and verify that they were at the doctor's office as many times as was listed," Shiller said.

He also stressed that the settlement is not an admission of guilt, and is for an amount "far less than we would have spent to try it (the case) before a jury."

> CSAA settled the case after two days of a trial that lawyers had expected to last almost a year. The amount of the settlement was confidential, but sources said it totalled more than $4 million.

In general, though, suing insurance is difficult. The standard auto insurance policy addresses the matter of when, and under what conditions, **legal action** may be taken against the insurance company to recover on a claim.

> For example, if coverage applies and the insurer does not pay a legitimate claim, the claimant may sue the insurance company, but only after there has been compliance with the conditions specified in this section.

No person has any right to sue the company until the company has agreed in writing that you have a legal obligation to pay the claimant or a judgment against you has been made in court. No one has a right to take legal action against the company in order to determine your liability.

REGULATORY REFORM ISSUES

In 1993, California Insurance Commissioner John Garamendi put in place a number of **regulations** to simplify the claims process.

The California regulations were loosely patterned after model standards adopted in 1991 by the National Association of Insurance Commissioners. Insurance industry analysts predicted their use in California may influence other states' treatment of **similar standards**.

> Increasingly, though, auto insurance companies look at all the lawsuits as reason to pay claims quickly.

Among Garamendi's 1993 regulations:

- Within 15 days of any **notice of claim**, an insurance company must acknowledge receiving the notice. The company must also start its investigation within 15 days of receiving a notice of claim.
- Within 40 days of receiving a notice of claim, an insurance company must af-

firm or deny the claim and affirm or deny liability.

- If 40 days isn't sufficient time, the company must write to the claimant and specify **why more time is needed**, and **what further information** it needs.

- A **denial** of a policyholder's claim, in whole or in part, must be accompanied by a letter that spells out the **policy provisions and factors** on which the company is relying. All written denials must include a notice that the company's decision can be reviewed by the Insurance Department, and must provide the department's address and phone number.

- Insurance companies must disclose to their policyholders all **benefits, coverage, time limits** or other relevant provisions of any policy they have issued that may apply to a claim.

- "Any other communication" that "reasonably suggests that a response is expected," and that regards a claim not in litigation, must be responded to **within 15 days** of receipt.

Garamendi said that **stringent regulatory efforts** would help insurance companies improve their **customer service** as well as significantly drive down the number of justified complaints filed with the department in 1993.

> A justified complaint is one that involves a violation of the Insurance Code or other insurance laws, or one in which the consumer was unable to get an insurer to respond to his or her concerns of questions. Typical complaints involve delay of payment on claims, disputes on amounts owed to policyholders by their insurance companies and misrepresentation of coverage purchased.

CONCLUSION

When they think about making insurance claims, most people worry about following all the rules for reporting an accident, theft or other loss. These rules are important—but fairly straightforward.

What you should be thinking of when you make a claim is getting the maximum payment in the minimum time. In order to do this, you have to keep in mind how insurance companies think of claims. They usually handle claims in a systematic, impersonal manner. Their biggest concerns are not paying more than they have to and not getting sued.

This said, most insurance companies will settle claims fairly quickly—once they've been made.

But making your claim in a timely manner isn't the end of the process. The settlement your company offers can be negotiated. If you keep track of the expenses and losses you've incurred, you'll usually be in a decent position to argue for more coverage if you feel it's owed.

HOW TO MAKE AN INSURANCE CLAIM

CHAPTER 12

COMMON PROBLEMS—AND HOW TO AVOID THEM

Whether you're shopping for auto insurance, making a claim or negotiating a settlement, there are a number of common problems that plague the auto insurance process. Understanding these problems gives you the best chance to anticipate and avoid them. And, if you can't avoid them, it helps you find a quick solution.

EXCLUSIONS

Exclusions identify types of losses that are not covered by the policy. While the Insuring Agreement defines the coverage in broad terms by describing what is covered (like bodily injury and property damage resulting from accidents), the exclusions help to shape the coverage and narrow the scope of coverage by specifying **losses that the policy won't pay.**

> Exclusions form the basis of most of the legal disputes that occur between policyholders and insurance companies.

Exclusions are generally included in insurance policies to accomplish these four broad purposes:

- to **clarify the intent** of coverage;
- to remove coverages for losses which should be covered by **other forms of insurance**;
- to remove coverage for losses which result from **above-average risk factors** which are not anticipated in average rates and premiums (usually this coverage is available at an additional charge); and
- to remove coverage for **catastrophic losses** which are generally not insurable (although coverage may be available through special insurance pools or government programs).

An insured person who uses an automobile to **intentionally injure** another person or damage property is not covered since, in most cases, these acts would be of a criminal nature and against public policy to cover them.

No coverage is provided for damage to any property of others in your possession. If you backed over a lawn mower borrowed from a neighbor, there would be no coverage. Note that this exclusion does not apply (therefore, coverage is granted) for property damage to **residences or garages you don't own.**

There is no coverage for injuries to an **employee** injured while working for you. But injury to a domestic employee would be covered if workers compensation for domestics was not required or available.

CHAPTER 12

The standard policy excludes coverage for the liability of any person while a vehicle is being used as a public or livery conveyance. This exclusion is designed both to clarify the intent of coverage and to exclude something that should be covered by other insurance. (Anyone who operates a taxi or limousine service and carries passengers for a fee needs a Business Auto Policy.)

> The livery exclusion does not apply to a share-the-expense car pool. When people participate in a **car pool** and only share the expenses for fuel, tolls and parking, the driver is not charging a fee for services.

Several exclusions eliminate coverage for something which should be covered by **another kind of insurance**. On-the-job injuries to employees are more properly covered under a Workers Compensation and Employers Liability policy (in fact, for most occupations, this coverage is required by state law). An employee injured on-the-job is generally eligible for workers compensation benefits, even if the injury resulted from an automobile accident.

> For example, if you took your car to a garage for repairs and an employee of the garage had an accident while road testing your car, there would be no coverage for the employee under your Personal Auto Policy (you would still be covered as the owner of the car).

COMMON PROBLEMS—AND HOW TO AVOID THEM

Some of the exclusions for **medical payments** are similar to those for liability coverage and others apply only to the medical payments. Among these:

- There is no coverage while occupying a vehicle having fewer than four wheels, such as a motorcycle.

- There is no coverage while occupying a vehicle used primarily as a residence. This might sound a bit unusual at first, but it makes more sense when you consider that some vans and pickups may be equipped to include living space. If a vehicle is used as a regular residence, then the medical coverage would amount to 24-hour health coverage.

Physical damage exclusions are numerous. A few of these exclude losses which are not insurable under a standard policy. But many of them simply exclude types of vehicles or equipment which represent an above-average risk which is not included in average rates and premiums. Among these:

- The policy will not pay for loss due to wear and tear and other kinds of losses that occur as a normal part of owning and using a vehicle. Because such losses are to be expected, they are not accidental and are therefore not covered by insurance.

- The policy eliminates coverage for losses caused by catastrophic exposures, similar to exclusions we found in the medical payments section.

- The policy generally excludes coverage for sound reproduction equipment (such as radios, stereos, tape players and compact disc players). It also excludes coverage for the accessories and media used with these (such as tapes, records and discs). However, this is one coverage which is available by endorsement for an extra charge.

> In recent years, this exclusion has been modified to reflect advances in modern technology. The exclusion applies to other electronic equipment which receives or transmits audio, visual or data signals. In earlier years, policies made no reference to "visual or data signals." But the exclusion now also applies to such devices as car telephones, television monitors, video cassette recorders (VCRs), and personal computers.

- There is no coverage for loss by confiscation or destruction by governmental authorities because the car is being used in illegal activities (e.g., transporting drugs), or for failure to comply with EPA (environmental) standards. The EPA item is aimed at "gray market" vehicles (shipped here illegally from other countries). Under both of these situations, the government can confiscate, and sometimes destroy the involved vehicles.

- There is no coverage for damage to a non-owned auto used by the insured or a family member unless there is a "reasonable belief" that the insured or family member is entitled to do so.

- The policy excludes coverage for devices that detect or locate radar or laser beams. These devices are used by some drivers to determine where the police have set up radar to help enforce the speed limit. Because the purpose of radar detectors is to help drivers avoid obeying speed laws, and because such equipment has been outlawed in some states, insurance companies are unwilling to provide coverages for these devices under an auto policy.

The standard Personal Auto Policy includes two additional exclusions:

- There will be no physical damage coverage for any auto located inside a racing facility for the purpose of competing in, or practicing or preparing for, any prearranged or organized racing or speed contest.

- Coverage applies to loss to a rental car only if the rental car company is prevented from seeking recovery from you or a family member under the terms of the rental agreement or under state law. In other words, the insurance company is not going to pay when you would not otherwise suffer a loss.

CHAPTER 12

OTHER INSURANCE

The standard policy's Other Insurance clause explains how the coverage will apply if there is other insurance covering the same loss. This is designed, in part, to prevent claimants from **profiting** from an accident by collecting the full amount of damages twice. It is also designed to allow insurance companies to settle claims in a fair and just manner, by permitting them to pay only their share of a loss when there is coverage under multiple policies.

As you might guess, disputes sometimes arise over how terms like *fair and just* and *only their share* are defined. But this dispute—like subrogation disputes we've considered elsewhere—are usually most important among insurance companies.

The language of the clause itself is pretty straightforward:

> If there is other applicable liability insurance we will pay only our share of the loss. Our share is the proportion that our limit of liability bears to the total of all applicable limits. However, any insurance we provide for a vehicle you do not own shall be excess over any other collectible insurance.

If valid insurance coverage is placed on an auto under two policies, then each company will pay its **proportionate share** of a claim. If one policy has a limit of $100,000 and another policy has a limit of $200,000, the total available would be $300,000, so one company would pay one-third and the other company would pay two-thirds of any liability claim.

With respect to coverage for any non-owned auto, your Personal Auto Policy applies as excess over any other collectible insurance.

NON-STANDARD RISKS

Having children who drive, getting tickets or being in several accidents may make you ineligible for the best rates a company offers. Normally companies divide auto policies into three categories—**preferred** for the best drivers with the least risk; **standard** for people with good but less than perfect records; and **non-standard** for high-risk drivers.

A typical purchaser of non-standard auto insurance often seeks minimum limits of liability required by law, has an undesirable or unverifiable driving record, poor credit history, poor claims experience, or minimal net worth.

In general, **personal credit ratings** are becoming an important element of rating auto insurance premiums. Most large insurance companies will use personal credit ratings as a secondary factor if a policy applicant meets some pre-determined risk profile.

More than a hundred American insurance companies use a credit test developed by Fair, Isaac & Co., a California-based statistical risk-evaluation firm. Other big companies—Allstate Insurance is one—use their own credit tests.

But how reliable are these tests? The companies say there's a clear connection between good credit risks and good insurance risks. They claim that people who don't pay their bills are more likely to file a theft, fire or accident claim.

Fair, Isaac & Co. evaluates at least 35 pieces of credit information. No single one makes a bad insurance risk. What matters is your total score. It includes how long you've had a credit card, the number of accounts that are 60 days past due, and any liens, judgments or bankruptcy filings. The test covers general credit information for the past five years and late-pay information for the past two years.

Allstate screens for several major credit blemishes incurred in the past five years, including foreclosures, judgments, bankruptcies and liens. It also looks for the second time you were subject to garnishment or repossession, or left a bill of $100 or more unpaid for at least three months. Just one of these problems can tip you into Allstate's high-risk company, which charges 50 percent to 100 percent more for coverage.

ENFORCING RELEASES

Sometimes, when you make claim on your auto insurance, the company will agree to pay if you sign a **release** freeing it from any further liability connected to your claim. Be extremely careful about signing any releases an insurance company offers.

The 1993 Arizona appeals court case *Bobby Sid Taylor v. State Farm Mutual Automobile Insurance Co.* shows how complicated a hastily-signed release can make an insurance claim.

The case began with an automobile accident that occurred in 1977. The accident involved three vehicles—

one occupied by Anne Ring and passenger James Rivers, the second by Douglas Wistrom, and the third by Taylor.

Ring, Rivers and Taylor all were injured. Ring, her husband and Rivers filed actions against Taylor and Wistrom. Taylor's insurer, State Farm, retained attorney Leroy W. Hofmann to defend Taylor. Taylor also personally retained attorney Norman Bruce Randall, who filed a counterclaim against Ring for Taylor's damages. Taylor, therefore, was represented by both Randall and Hofmann in the matter.

The Rings and Rivers settled with Wistrom before trial, so Taylor was the only party left facing the Ring/Rivers claims. At trial, the Rings and Rivers obtained combined verdicts against Taylor for approximately $2.5 million in excess of his insurance policy limits. The court of appeals affirmed the judgments.

The Rings eventually settled with State Farm. Taylor, however, sued State Farm for bad faith seeking damages for the excess Rivers judgment, claiming, among other things, that State Farm improperly failed to settle the Rivers matter within policy limits.

State Farm asked for a summary judgment, claiming that Taylor relinquished his bad faith claim when, in 1981, he signed a release drafted by attorney Randall in exchange for State Farm's payment of $15,000 in uninsured motorists benefits.

The release Taylor signed read, in its entirety:

CHAPTER 12

This Agreement made and entered into this 4th day of August, 1981, by and between BOBBY SID TAYLOR and the STATE FARM MUTUAL AUTOMOBILE INSURANCE COMPANY, (hereinafter referred to as STATE FARM), by and through its agent undersigned.

WHEREAS, BOBBY SID TAYLOR was covered by an automobile insurance policy issued by STATE FARM, which was in effect on the 9th day of April, 1977, providing liability and uninsured motorists coverage to him, and

WHEREAS, an automobile collision occurred on April 9, 1977 between vehicles operated by BOBBY SID TAYLOR, DOUGLAS ALAN WISTROM and ANNE L. RING, and

WHEREAS, a trial took place in the Superior Court of Maricopa County, State of Arizona in consolidated causes C-382960 and C383090, resulting in a jury verdict against BOBBY SID TAYLOR in the total amount of $2,621,000, and judgments having been entered against BOBBY SID TAYLOR in accordance with said jury verdicts, and

WHEREAS, having been fully apprised of all settlement offers made by the plaintiffs in the consolidated cases referred to above, during the discovery process, prior to trial, during the trial, and subsequently, BOBBY SID TAYLOR maintained and does now maintain that the operation of his motor vehicle on April 9, 1977 did not contribute to the injuries sustained by the plaintiffs, and at no time has he insisted, demanded, or even encouraged his insurer to settle the plaintiffs' claims within his policy limits, and

WHEREAS, one of the drivers of an automobile involved in the collision on April 9, 1977, to wit: DOUGLAS ALAN WISTROM, was uninsured on the date of said collision, and BOBBY SID TAYLOR having a bona fide belief that the negligence of DOUGLAS ALAN WISTROM contributed to his bodily injuries sustained in that collision, and

WHEREAS, BOBBY SID TAYLOR has demanded compensation from STATE FARM under the uninsured motorists coverage afforded to him, and

WHEREAS, BOBBY SID TAYLOR desires to settle the uninsured motorist claim, and to relieve STATE FARM of any and all other contractual claims, interests, or causes of action he has or may have against STATE FARM, and

WHEREAS, STATE FARM has agreed that uninsured motorists coverage is available to BOBBY SID TAYLOR and appropriate under the facts surrounding the collision on April 9, 1977, and STATE FARM having been fully apprised in the premises,

THEREFORE, in consideration of the mutual covenants contained herein, STATE FARM agrees to pay the sum of $15,000 to BOBBY SID TAYLOR in full satisfaction of all contractual rights, claims, and causes of action he has or may have against STATE FARM under the policy of insurance referred to herein, in connection with the collision on April 9, 1977, and all subsequent matters, and BOBBY SID TAYLOR hereby accepts that sum pursuant to the recitals contained herein.

CHAPTER 12

Having been instructed on the interpretation of the release, the jury returned a verdict in favor of Taylor for compensatory damages of $2.1 million. The court also awarded Taylor $300,000 in attorney fees.

The court of appeals reversed, holding that the release agreement was not ambiguous and therefore the judge erred by admitting evidence to vary its terms.

According to the court, because the release should have been strictly enforced, there was no basis for Taylor's bad faith claim. Taylor appealed.

The state supreme court wrote:

> ...Taylor released "all contractual rights, claims, and causes of action he ha[d] or may have against State Farm under the policy of insurance...in connection with the collision...and all subsequent matters."
>
> ...the release satisfies "all contractual rights, claims, and causes of action." As a matter of statutory or contract construction, the word "contractual" modifies the words "rights," "claims," and the words "causes of action."
>
> ...It is reasonable to believe that if the parties had agreed to release the bad faith claim, they would not have drawn the release so narrowly—confining it to "contractual" and "subsequent" matters, with no mention of tort claims or bad faith.
>
> Surely, State Farm knew what language would effectively release it from Taylor's potential bad faith claim. It can be inferred that

> sophisticated parties in the business of settling insurance claims, faced with the task of releasing a claim as large as Taylor's, would have used more specific or at least broader language if that was their agreement.
>
> ...For these reasons, we hold that extrinsic evidence produces support for Taylor's contention that the release language was not intended to release his bad faith claim.

The trial jury had resolved the release issue in Taylor's favor. The high court left that resolution undisturbed.

CANCELLATION PROCEDURES

The last important factor in understanding how auto insurance works is the issue of **cancellation**. One of the most common complaints people make about car insurance is how quickly insurance companies will drop someone who has an accident or gets some tickets.

In May 1994, Georgia Insurance Commissioner Tim Ryles ordered Allstate Insurance Co. to pay a $3.547 million fine for violating insurance department auto cancellation rules.

The Allstate nonrenewal notice failed to inform policyholders about the reasons for nonrenewal, the availability of the state auto insurance assigned risk plan, the date coverage was to be terminated, as well as their right to contact the department for assistance.

"The policies for which the notices [of nonrenewal on standard auto policies] were issued were nonrenewed for valid and legal reasons," Allstate spokesman Al Orendorff told one insurance industry trade journal. "...we believe that Allstate's nonrenewal notice substantially complied with the state's statutory nonrenewal requirements."

In early 1995, Washington state Insurance Commissioner Deborah Senn announced a package of proposed laws, changes in procedure and consumer education programs to help people deal with auto insurance. The Washington reform package is a good example of the kind of consumer-oriented reform going on around the United States.

The centerpiece of the Washington package was a proposed law which would stop insurance companies from dropping or denying auto coverage based on a single accident per insured driver or because of accidents that aren't the fault of the insured.

> Insurance regulators hear many consumer complaints that insurance companies arbitrarily assigned partial blame to policyholders when accidents aren't their fault. After assigning blame without consulting the policyholder, some companies then cancel the coverage.

Another Washington proposal would prohibit insurance companies from denying people auto coverage because coverage was previously canceled or denied by another company. Consumer groups call the practice **blacklisting**.

COMMON PROBLEMS—AND HOW TO AVOID THEM

A growing number of policyholders complain that, if they make even a small claim, insurance companies will threaten to cancel their coverage unless they buy other insurance policies—like homeowners or umbrella liability.

> When an insurance company cancels your policy, it usually has to tell you why it's done so. Some states require that the insurance company offer you alternative coverage—usually at a higher cost.

If your policy is canceled, the insurance company has to **refund** part of whatever premium you've already paid. The refund is calculated on a **pro rata basis**, which means an even distribution of the premium based on the time coverage was in effect.

On the other hand, there are situations where a return premium computation is not based on an even division of the premium, and the insurance company is allowed to retain slightly more than a pro rata share in order to recover the expenses of issuing the policy. When a policy is issued, the insurance company expects to recover its **administrative expenses** of typing up the policy and keeping policy records over the entire term of the policy.

When a policy is canceled early, the exposure to loss terminates but some of the insurer's fixed expenses remain the same. The insurer recovers these expenses by deducting a slight **penalty** from the return premium. Return premium calculations which include this penalty are often referred to as **short rate cancellations**.

For policy cancellations requested by you, the insurer usually returns only 90 percent of the pro rata portion of the unearned premium for the first policy year (thus, the penalty is 10 percent). This applies to **annual policies**, and to policies having a **shorter term**, such as three or six months.

If a **two or three year policy** is canceled during the first year, the insurer will usually return **90 percent** of the pro rata unearned premium for the first year plus the **full premium** for any subsequent periods. If a two or three year policy is canceled after the first year, the first year premium is fully earned, the initial expenses have been recovered, and the insurer will return the full pro rata unearned premium for the unexpired term.

The cancellation penalty does not apply in all cases where you request cancellation.

Determining the pro rata portion of an annual premium is a simple procedure. You simply convert dates to decimal equivalents, and subtract the **effective date** from the **cancellation date**. The result is then multiplied by the full annual premium to determine the **earned premium**—the amount to be retained by the company. The difference, or unearned premium, is the amount returned to the insured in full or to be reduced by 10 percent if the short rate penalty applies.

The **termination provision** is the longest of the General Provisions in the standard policy. It addresses the issues of when, how, and for what reasons coverage under a Personal Auto Policy can be terminated.

> This provision often varies from state to state. Check any applicable endorsements to determine whether there are any variations of the policy provisions relating to cancellation.

You may cancel the policy by either returning the policy or giving the company advance notice to cancel as of a certain date. The company's rights to cancel are more restrictive. It may cancel:

- For failure to pay the premium with 10 days notice to the insured.

- If the policy is new to the company (not a renewal or continuation), it may be canceled within the first 60 days with 10 days notice. For renewal or continuation policies, 20 days notice is required.

- After the policy has been in effect for 60 days, the insurer may cancel only:

    a. For nonpayment of premium.

    b. If the driver's license of the insured, any resident of the household, or any person who regularly uses the auto is suspended or revoked during the policy period. If the policy is for a period of less than one year, the policy period would start with the date of the last anniversary.

> c. *If the policy was obtained through material misrepresentation.*

The standard policy also presents the provisions that apply to **nonrenewal of a policy**. Insurance companies can have many different reasons for deciding not to renew an automobile insurance policy when it comes up for renewal.

> For example, the company might decide not to renew a policy because of accidents, traffic violations, or other factors which make it an undesirable risk, but for which midterm cancellation is not permitted. Or a company might decide to write fewer auto policies in the state and to write more commercial fire policies instead.

If the company decides not to renew the policy, it must notify you at least 20 days in advance of expiration. If the policy term is less than six months, the company has the right not to renew the policy every six months. If the policy term is other than one year, it may only exercise this right on an anniversary date.

It also describes conditions under which automatic termination of coverage will occur. The policy terminates automatically if you fail to accept the company's offer by paying the renewal premium. Coverage for any specific auto terminates as soon as any other similar insurance for that auto takes effect.

A final set of provisions is titled Other Termination Provisions. Here the policy specifies several miscellaneous conditions relating to cancellation or nonrenewal.

- Proof of mailing notice of cancellation or nonrenewal is proof that proper notice has been given to the insured. The company may deliver the notice instead of mailing it.

- The company agrees to refund any unearned premium to the insured if the policy is canceled.

- The cancellation date on the notice becomes the expiration date of the policy.

NEGLIGENT ENTRUSTMENT

The 1994 Louisiana case *Carolyn Sue Panzico (for Jennifer Powell) v. Dianne Price, et al.* considered some complicated family connections and another often-disputed issue—**negligent entrustment**. This issue relates particularly to the insurance issues raised when you **lend someone your car**.

In January 1989, a car driven by Danny Knight struck Jennifer Powell, who was standing in a parking lot in Monroe, Louisiana. Powell was seriously injured.

The car belonged to Dianne Price, the named insured on the State Farm policy that covered the vehicle. Price had given her minor stepson, Shane, permission to use her car that evening for a date. When his date was canceled, Shane picked up Danny Knight and the two boys went for a ride. They eventually parked the car and stood visiting with friends. Shane gave Danny permission to borrow the car to drive to a nearby A&P parking lot, where he hit Powell.

Danny was sixteen years old at the time of the accident. Police investigation of the accident revealed that he did not have a driver's license. Shane, however, was not aware that Danny was without a license. He had seen Danny driving in the past and assumed that, because he was old enough to obtain a license, he had one.

Jennifer Powell's mother, Carolyn Panzico, filed suit on behalf of her daughter for damages—mostly relating to back injuries—arising from the accident.

Danny Knight, his father and State Farm Fire and Casualty Insurance Company were formally dismissed as defendants following a private settlement. The remaining defendants were Dianne Price, her son Shane and State Farm Mutual Automobile Insurance Company.

Dianne Price and Shane both testified that he had very limited access to Dianne's vehicle. The keys were unavailable to him. He had to seek special permission and state his purpose each time he wanted to borrow the car. If permission was granted, Shane was reminded not to drink and drive or to allow anyone else to drive the car. Price was unaware that Shane previously let his friends drive the car.

The trial court concluded that Danny was not covered under Dianne Price's insurance policy because it was not reasonably foreseeable to Price that Shane would lend her car to a third driver. It also found the claim of negligent entrustment lacked merit because the evidence was not sufficient to establish that Shane negligently entrusted Danny with Price's car.

Furthermore, the court found that if there had been any negligence, it was strictly in Danny's operation of the vehicle, not in Shane's lending the car to him. Powell appealed.

The appeals court ruled:

The trial court determined that Price could not have reasonably foreseen that Shane would lend the car to another person. Price restricted Shane's use [of the car] to specific occasions, always subject to the restriction that he not drink and drive or allow anyone else to use the car....

The *Price* court found a **reasonable foreseeability test** compelling. In explaining this test, it cited an earlier state supreme court decision:

> Implying permission, as in other contractual implications, is nothing less than a judicial extension of the terms of an obligation by reading into the language a meaning which is not clearly expressed. It is, in effect, a rewriting of the contract between the parties....It is an authority to be most carefully exercised calling for a proper restraint by courts.

In the late 1980s, a number of state court decisions had proceeded to imply exactly this permission. The Louisiana supreme court had itself interpreted some insurance policies in this way. In the decision *Norton v. Lewis*, it chose to use the word "permission" in the **broadest sense possible**. It held that:

> Once the permission, whether express or implied, to use a motor vehicle is established it is given a wide and liberal meaning in determining coverage. So long as the initial use of the vehicle is with the consent, express or implied, of the insured, any subsequent changes in the character or scope of the use do not require additional specific consent of the insured; coverage will be precluded only where the deviation from the use consented to amounts to theft or other conduct displaying utter disregard for the return or safekeeping of the vehicle.

> **Though the Louisiana courts contradicted this theory in the *Price* decision, many courts might stand by it. So, be careful to whom you lend your car.**

CONCLUSION

There are more situations that can cause problems in a policy or claim than we've considered in this chapter—but these are the most common grounds for dispute.

As you can see in the examples, most problems with insurance don't surface until you make a claim which is denied or underpaid. These responses from the insurance company make people angry—but they're usually a result of misperceptions or confusion which occurred much earlier.

So, the best way to avoid the problems *later* is to read your policy carefully and know the trouble spots *sooner*.

CHAPTER 13

FRAUD

It's a reality of the modern insurance market that unwitting consumers get ripped off. In many markets, the rip-offs focus on selling **multiple, redundant policies**. In auto insurance, the two biggest scams are selling **policies written by insurance companies that are bankrupt or don't exist** and adding **bogus surcharges** to premium bills.

In August 1995, the owner of a south Florida insurance agency was arrested and charged criminally with bilking more than 1,000 customers out of nearly $100,000 by slipping unneeded or **unwanted charges** into their auto policies.

Months later in north Florida, four agents working for another insurance agency in its Tallahassee and Pensacola offices were charged in administrative complaints in what investigators said was a similar scheme.

In each instance, the agents allegedly ripped off consumers through a deceptive sales scheme known in industry jargon as **sliding**.

Besides the cases resulting in charges, investigators with the Florida Department of Insurance had a number of other sliding allegations under active investigation.

> Insurance department investigators in other heavily-populated states—including California, Texas, New Jersey and New York—have begun campaigns to stamp out sliding.

THE COST OF HARD-SELL TACTICS

The main benefit of charting various quotes is that it makes **resisting hard-sell sales tactics** easier. The 1994 Illinois appeals court decision *Steven Golembiewski v. Hallberg Insurance Agency, Inc.* illustrates just how complicated basic auto insurance can get when aggressive agents use hard-sell tactics.

In August 1988 Steven Golembiewski contacted Mark Zintak, who was associated with the Hallberg Insurance Agency and "requested that he be bound with automobile insurance coverage."

Golembiewski had just bought a 1985 Chevrolet Camaro for $9,200. He had financed the car, so he needed to obtain collision and liability insurance to meet the terms of his loan. His father had recommended Hallberg.

Zintak took down his "information...driver's license number, and address." Zintak sent Golembiewski an application in the mail. Zintak told him to fill in the "highlighted areas."

CHAPTER 13

Two days later, Golembiewski called Zintak again and said, "[T]he lady from the finance company had called and that I would have to have insurance today....I told him that I must have insurance today, I must be binded. I did not know what binded was."

> Being binded means to be temporarily insured while an application is processed.

Zintak told Golembiewski that he could consider himself covered immediately and that he should send the signed application and a check for $225 immediately.

Early the next morning, Golembiewski sent a check for $225 to Hallberg Insurance Agency. On the application, he only filled in the highlighted portions; he did not know who filled in the rest of the information on it. At trial, he looked at the application and noted that there was another signature by the line marked "producer."

When he called the automobile dealership to inform it that he had procured insurance, Golembiewski said that Kemper was his insurance company and Hallberg was his agent. He told the dealership that he had coverage for liability and collision.

Two days later, Golembiewski was involved in an automobile accident. He contacted Zintak and notified him of the accident. Zintak put him on hold for a few moments and then told him that he wasn't covered for the accident. Hallberg had not received his check—

therefore, his insurance coverage had not come into effect yet.

Golembiewski sued Hallberg and Zintak, alleging a breach of contract and a consumer fraud claim. (Golembiewski eventually dismissed Zintak from the case.)

The trial judge ultimately directed verdicts in favor of Golembiewski on the breach of contract and consumer fraud claims. She entered judgment in the amount of $6,811.03, which included the $4000 amount that Golembiewski paid to the other driver, interest on the loan he took out to pay her and the cost of repairing his own car.

On the consumer fraud claim, the judge did not make any separate award, but she did assess $4,000 in attorney fees against Hallberg, based on the Consumer Fraud and Deceptive Business Practices Act.

Hallberg appealed, making various arguments. The appeals court reviewed records of the case in an exceptionally detailed manner. It supported the trial court on almost every count.

The award to Golembiewski stood, though he had to pay his own attorney fees. Hallberg tried to place him with a substandard insurance company, so he went with another agency.

POLICY PROVISIONS

The standard auto policy refuses to cover any sort of fraudulent claims:

CHAPTER 13

> We do not provide coverage for any "insured" who has made fraudulent statements or engaged in fraudulent conduct in connection with any accident or loss for which coverage is sought under this policy.

This provision, which is very brief, deals with voiding the insurance coverage in cases where a **policyholder has committed fraud**. Other insured persons involved in the same accident are not affected by this provision, as long as they are not guilty of fraud themselves.

The insurance company is under no obligation to honor the policy when the insured's actions or statements in connection with an accident are dishonest.

So-called "California-style," auto insurance claims operations have defrauded insurance companies of hundreds of millions of dollars nationwide. A high volume of low-priced insurance claims for staged accidents or exaggerated injuries.

California has toughened laws on insurance fraud and tightened its regulatory controls of the affected professions, so many of the sharpest operators have moved on to other states. Wherever they are, these crooks exploit one basic trend.

"Most companies, including State Farm, had a figure under which they wouldn't bother to even question a claim," says a former State Farm investigator. "In most cases, that was about $5,000—although it can vary with different adjusters."

Although an insurance company may see a pattern of suspicious claims handled by certain attorneys or physicians, it has to treat each claim individually—or face charges of bad faith.

INSURANCE COMPANY RESPONSE

Finally, one of the coverage issues that insurance companies pursue most aggressively is suspected **fraud**. If a company even thinks that a claim might be bogus, it will delay—and perhaps deny—any coverage.

"**Every American household** is burdened with **more than $200 annually** in additional insurance premiums to make up for this type of fraud," said FBI Director Louis Freeh in a 1995 press release. "Staged automobile accidents are a major contributor to the more than $20 billion a year property and casualty insurance fraud problem—out of an estimated $70 billion to $80 billion a year in health care fraud—and illustrate the subversion of the American health care system by unscrupulous medical providers and their partners in crime."

The 1994 Massachusetts appeals court decision *Ricardo Guity v. Commerce Insurance Company* illustrates why auto carriers often suspect fraud.

Guity had reported his automobile, a 1985 BMW 745I, stolen on November 6, 1988, from a shopping mall while he was watching a movie.

When he had applied for automobile insurance, Guity had given as his address that of his parents in the Hyde Park section of Boston, rather than his own in the Mattapan section. His application for insurance made in May, 1988, listed an odometer reading of 29,900 miles, but the vehicle, when found after its reported theft, showed an odometer with 29,449 miles on it.

The car when found had been vandalized, a total wreck, yet the ignition system, door locks, and trunk lock were intact. Guity claimed to have paid $25,000 for his BMW, but documents filed with the Registry of Motor Vehicles stated a sales price of $11,500. Documents of the United States Customs Service estimated a value of $5,866.67, apparently owing to the vehicle's nonconformance with applicable environmental specifications.

At a certain point Guity had allowed his insurance to lapse and when he reapplied for insurance in October 1988, one month before he reported his car stolen, he listed mileage of 31,000 miles.

Commerce Insurance promptly began investigation of the reported theft. Its investigator, Franklin Jones, experienced some difficulty in catching up with Guity. When he finally did make contact, Jones asked Guity for an affidavit and to conduct a taped interview. Guity provisionally declined either affidavit or interview until he talked to his lawyer. When Jones pressed his requests, Guity responded that he had spoken to his lawyer and would neither put anything in writing nor submit to a tape recorded interview.

The applicable insurance policy, the standard Massachusetts form, provided in connection with claims procedures:

> If you are filing a claim for damage to your auto, you or someone on your behalf must file a proof of loss within 91 days after the accident.

> We may also require you to submit to an examination under oath.
>
> After an accident or loss, you...must cooperate with us in the investigation, settlement and defense of any claim or lawsuit....

By letter dated March 13, 1989, Commerce denied coverage because of Guity's failure to cooperate and the submission of false documents at the time of purchasing his insurance. Commerce also declined settlement in response to a letter from Guity's lawyer.

Guity sued, claiming two points: breach of the insurance contract and the violation of state law on unfair settlement practice (which would automatically triple any award made from the first charge).

The contract claim was tried and submitted to a jury, which found that: Guity had not made material misrepresentations either in applying for the Commerce policy or in his claim of loss for his BMW; he had not failed to cooperate with Commerce's investigation of the claimed theft; and that the cash value of the car before the loss had been $18,075.

The trial judge then heard supplementary evidence on the triple damages claim. On the basis of that evidence, as well as the evidence she had heard at the proceedings before the jury, she ruled against Guity. More specifically, she wrote that:

> Commerce began the investigation of Guity's claimed loss reasonably promptly....Commerce thereafter proceeded with reasonable efficiency and thoroughness in its investigation, and promptly informed Guity (by letter

dated November 28, 1988) that...[he] was failing to cooperate with the investigation. Guity did fail to cooperate by declining or refusing to be interviewed or to fill out any affidavit describing the loss.

Guity appealed, pressing for the triple damages. The appeals court considered the words of the unfair settlement practices statute:

[A]n unfair claim settlement practice shall consist of any of the following acts or omissions:

...Compelling insureds to institute litigation to recover amounts due under an insurance policy by offering substantially less than the amounts ultimately recovered in actions brought by such insureds.

The appeals court agreed with the trial court that there was more to this case than just low-balling a claim. In the face of Guity's failure to cooperate, the evidence that the theft of the BMW may have been contrived, and the inflation of the purchase price on Guity's claim, the company reasonably and promptly notified him of the reasons for declining payment on the policy. There was no unfair settlement practice.

So, insurance companies have good reason to suspect fraud. According to the FBI, **typical cases** involve one of several scenarios:

- **Caused accidents** in which an innocent victim can be made an unwitting participant in an actual accident, such as a sideswiping (law enforcement people call this scam "swoop and squat").

- **Staged accidents** in which vehicles with prior damage are brought together and made to appear to have been involved in an accident.

- **Paper accidents** in which no accident occurred but false accident reports were filed to support insurance claims.

- So-called **phantom vehicle claims**, in which motorists claim to have suffered a loss from a hit-and-run driver who does not exist.

- **Personal-injury mills**, in which lawyers and physicians—some working alone, some working together—submit claims for patients' nonexistent or exaggerated injuries.

- Cars **abandoned by owners** hoping to cash in on the theft coverage in their insurance policies.

Historically, based on a financial decision to avoid expensive trials, insurance companies have agreed to settle suspect medical and auto damage claims. But that's changing. These scams—especially the "swoop and squat" claims—have become a coast-to-coast problem.

Solo drivers—more often women—and tourists are the favorite targets of **swoop and squat** teams. As a result, rental car companies and large insurance companies have been hit with millions of dollars in false claims.

Law enforcement agencies have also clamped down on the more **organized insurance fraud** rings.

In the fall of 1995, the U.S. Attorney in Boston announced that chiropractor Alan Rosenthal of Wellesley, Massachusetts, had been convicted of insurance fraud and would serve a 15-month term of imprisonment. In addition to the prison term, Rosenthal faced a criminal fine of $300,906.61 which would have to be paid by the end of 1995 and $129,093.39 in restitution.

Caterina Rosenthal, the chiropractor's wife, was sentenced to a two-year term of probation. As part of a plea agreement, she also relinquished her interest in assets jointly held with her husband.

The Rosenthals defrauded automobile and workers' compensation insurers by overstating patients' injuries and by running-up patients' bills with unnecessary tests and treatments. Their business, which at its peak employed as many as six "associate" chiropractors and numerous clerical employees, was almost entirely dependent on referrals from personal injury lawyers.

To build and sustain the business, the Rosenthals prepared reports for use by lawyers negotiating insurance settlements in which virtually all automobile and workers' compensation patients were found to suffer periods of total or partial disability, regardless of whether the patients' medical records supported such findings.

In addition, the Rosenthals made sure that virtually every automobile accident patient who came to their clinic received a high enough bill to get over the $2,000 "no-fault" lawsuit threshold. (Under Massachusetts' "no-fault" auto insurance laws, people who claim to have been injured in car accidents are entitled to have their medical bills paid, but those who claim so-called "soft-tissue" injuries, such as "whiplash," cannot bring lawsuits for "pain and suffering" damages unless their medical bills exceed $2,000.)

The Rosenthals' false reports helped lawyers obtain larger settlements than they could have if patient's true medical condition had been reported and their excessive testing and treatment enabled lawyers to bring lawsuits that would otherwise have been barred if the Rosenthals had not run the bills up over $2,000.

In order to pad bills, Alan Rosenthal instituted policies designed to ensure unnecessary and excessive testing and treatment of patients. He also required that all automobile accident and workers' compensation patients undergo at least 25 office visits, regardless of the patients' injuries or needs.

Three months earlier, in June 1995, state and local investigators in Los Angeles had cracked a major auto insurance fraud ring based in a Hollywood insurance agency where uninsured drivers who had car accidents could obtain **back dated insurance policies**.

The suspected ringleaders were Samuel Nadjarian and Khatchik Sahakian, partners in Red Light Insurance Services. Investigators said the two men, for a $1,000 fee, would supply uninsured motorists with auto insurance policies back dated to the date of their car accidents or a few days before so that the drivers could file claims for medical bills and damage to their vehicles.

Policies written under the California Assigned Risk Plan are randomly distributed to individual insurance companies based on their California market share. That aspect made it harder for insurers to spot a pattern in the claims than if only one or two companies had been victimized, investigators said. But they did begin to solve the case with information provided from insurance companies disputing coverage.

Sahakian and Nadjarian were suspected of back dating policies since 1992, if not earlier. The fraudulent claims—which ranged from a little more than $1,000 to a high of $35,000—totaled $410,000, investigators said.

BAD FAITH

Lawsuits or regulatory complaints relating to delays or denials usually allege **bad faith** on the part of the insurance company. This is one of the heaviest clubs a policyholder can wield to strike back at an insurance company.

One way in which an insurance company can act in bad faith is by **not investigating a claim** with an eye toward providing coverage.

In January 1995, State Farm Mutual Automobile Insurance Co.—the largest provider of auto insurance in Arizona—was ordered to pay $910,000 to a family after a jury found that the company acted in bad faith on an accident claim.

FRAUD

Three children in the Ahring family were injured in a head-on collision in 1989. The ownership of the truck in which they were riding was in dispute, and State Farm was accused of failing to disclose a memo that would have cleared up ownership.

According to John Osborne, a lawyer for the Ahrings, the pickup was a loaner from a garage to the children's grandfather, Milburn Sherwood. Osborne described Sherwood as senile and said that after the wreck, the garage owner insisted that the grandfather had bought the truck.

The point was important, because the other driver, who was at fault, did not have insurance. Because it was initially thought that the grandfather owned the truck, the family collected under his uninsured motorists insurance, provided by State Farm.

But the family would have been much better off collecting under the garage's policies, which provided higher coverage. The garage's uninsured motorists coverage was through Truck Insurance Exchange.

The family sued State Farm after a memo was discovered at a State Farm agent's office clearly indicating that the garage owned the truck. The family's lawyers alleged that State Farm was motivated to hide the memo because of confusion over whether it might be liable (among other things, it had issued an umbrella liability policy to the garage).

Steve Smith, a lawyer representing State Farm, said the verdict would be appealed. Smith said the memo was never hidden and proved nothing. He said the jury was swayed by the injuries suffered by the Ahring children.

"This is a very **liberal standard** against the insurance companies. It is probably the most liberal, compared to other states who require either malice or the absence of any reasonable basis," says one attorney. "We could have a bad faith claim based only on delay, and all the worry, grief and turmoil caused. This was the first important result of this case, because insurers think that **as long as they ultimately pay up**, it doesn't matter how long they drag it out."

CONCLUSION

Fraud is more than just a problem for people who are ripped off by criminals. It pervades insurance, surfacing as everything from hard-sell sales tactics to questionable or inflated claims to the sale of bogus policies. It affects the day-to-day relationship between insurance companies and even their honest customers.

As a smart consumer, you want to avoid getting ripped off. But you also want to make sure that your legitimate coverage—and claims when you make them—aren't undermined by an environment of fraud. You can best do this by dealing with established people and companies, using some discretion when you drive and reporting fraud whenever you have grounds to suspect it.

FRAUD

INDEX

accidents 1-6, 9, 10-18, 23-28, 31, 36, 38, 40, 45, 48, 51, 53-59, 62-65, 71-72, 79-80, 82, 86, 89-101, 104-108, 113, 114, 117, 119-120, 122-124, 127, 129-130, 134-135, 147, 149-150, 154-157, 159, 163, 165-166, 173, 177-180, 186-188, 193-197, 203-204, 207, 209, 213, 215, 217-218, 221-223, 228-229, 233, 235, 241-251
   fatal accidents 5
   injury accidents 5
actual cash value (ACV) 38, 59, 61, 137, 139, 140
additional insured 139
adjuster 147, 154, 193, 205-206
age 5, 22-26, 33-34, 37, 40-41, 81, 157, 166, 172, 177-183, 185, 187-188
alcohol 36
alternative markets 56
American Association of Retired Persons (AARP) 179-180
American Bar Association 172
application 4, 59, 167, 184, 191, 240-241, 244
appraisal 60-61
   appraiser 60-61, 147
arbitration 61, 112-113
assets 28-29, 31, 43, 72, 93, 102, 127, 149, 249
assigned risk 56-59, 251
at fault 2, 51, 89-90, 165, 252
automobile classifications 174
bad faith 224, 227-228, 244, 251, 253
bailee 82-83

bankruptcy (bankrupt) 61-62, 223, 239
benefit 2-3, 14, 17-18, 31, 44, 53-54, 81-83, 97, 104, 106, 118-120, 122, 126, 128-129, 135, 155, 217, 224, 240
bond 9, 108, 203-204
bound 107, 240
broker 145, 146, 174
business use 32, 187-188
California Department of Insurance 103
California Highway Patrol 5
cancellation 84, 178, 228, 231-234
car pool 110, 156, 217
cash 9, 29, 59-61, 114, 129, 137, 139-140, 163, 200, 205, 246, 248
Change Endorsement 41, 133, 136
claim 4, 7-9, 13, 16-18, 27, 32, 44, 47, 51-52, 55, 57-59, 64-65, 70-71, 82, 88, 92, 96-100, 105-106, 110, 113-114, 117, 119-130, 143, 146-147, 149, 160-161, 163, 166, 193-215, 221-230, 236-237, 242-253
   catastrophic (claim) 53, 125, 216, 218
   claims experience 125, 222
   claims paying 7
collision 2, 10, 12-13, 15-17, 25, 30, 32, 41-43, 55-56, 70, 77, 85-86, 104, 117, 150, 152, 155, 159-162, 164, 175, 177, 180-185, 205, 208, 225-227, 240-241, 252
collision damage waiver (CDW) 15-17
commercial lender 1
commission 7, 166
complaint 8, 154, 194, 209, 212-213, 228-229, 239, 251
computer on-line services 7
confiscation 219
consumer rights 146
Consumers Union 4

contents 76
contract 15, 33, 47, 70, 72, 73, 84, 100, 131, 142, 193, 227, 236, 242, 246
contractual terms 83
correspondence 194
cost containment 119, 148
counterfeit insurance card 104
coverage 2-35, 38-185, 196-233, 237, 240-246, 248, 251-253
   comprehensive 55, 184-185
   excess 65
crash involvement rate 5
current market value 29, 205
damages 2-3, 6, 11-12, 25, 31, 43, 56, 61, 65-66, 89-92, 95-101, 106, 107, 108, 111-114, 118, 120, 122, 128, 130, 163, 173, 199-204, 221, 224, 227, 235
   compensatory damages 97, 106-107, 227
   non-economic damages 128
   punitive damages 107
deceptive sales scheme 239
declarations page 36, 39-40, 42, 48, 69, 73, 83, 131, 133
declared value 34
deductible 2-3, 11-13, 16, 43, 150, 152, 159-160, 163, 170, 181, 185, 199-200, 205
defects 122
defense costs 96, 200-202
definitions 69, 71, 73, 78, 80, 83, 88
delaying payment 207
delivery 50, 75, 173
denial 208, 212, 251
direct mail 7, 146
disability 3, 18, 90, 97, 111, 155, 249
discount 35, 95, 155, 158, 165, 187-188
discrimination 24

INDEX

driver safety 23, 166
driver training 22, 177
driving record 1, 10, 24-25, 56, 81, 86-87, 148, 158, 171-172, 178, 186, 189, 190, 222
driving while intoxicated 25
drugs 122, 219
drunken driver 119
Duties after a Loss 196
Duties after an Accident 196
duty to defend 96, 202
earthquake 12
effective date 41, 48, 133, 231
eligibility 49, 173
employee 50, 81-82, 216-217, 249
endorsement 41-42, 62-63, 109, 131-143, 174, 177, 219, 232
exclusion 6, 26, 44, 45, 56, 84-88, 105, 110-111, 132, 136, 138, 215-220
expiration date 40, 48, 234
falling objects 12
family members 26, 44, 51, 74, 78
financial responsibility 9, 10, 108, 112-113, 134, 195, 199
fire 2, 12, 58, 83, 95, 159, 164-165, 223, 233
flood 2, 12, 95
forfeiture 197
fraud 129, 242-244, 247, 249-251, 253
freight 50, 75, 173
funeral benefit 3
garage 27, 83, 166, 204, 217, 252
    garaged car 27, 166
general provisions 61, 231
good student 22, 155, 158, 187-188
governmental authorities 219
Gross Vehicle Weight 50

hard-sell tactics 240
hazard 2, 122, 141
health insurance 31, 44, 120-121, 124, 147, 165, 208
hit-and-run accidents 27
household 4, 17, 25, 32-33, 49, 73-75, 80, 87, 142, 155-157, 186-187, 232, 244
illegal activities 219
income continuation benefit 18
indemnification 36, 62, 125
insurable interest 138-139
insurance agents 7, 145
insurance companies 4, 7-8, 22-27, 32, 35, 39, 50, 53-58, 64, 70, 76, 80, 82, 90-92, 114, 117, 121-122, 126, 133, 145, 147-150, 158, 160, 163-164, 170-174, 177-178, 181, 183-184, 189-190, 194, 196, 207-209, 211-213, 215, 220-222, 228-230, 239, 243-244, 247-248, 251, 253
  carriers 146, 157
Insurance Information Institute 145
Insurance Services Office (ISO) 9, 13, 23, 36, 55, 173, 176, 186
Insuring Agreement 16, 51, 84, 96, 106, 108, 111, 215
intangibles 90
intent of coverage 216-217
interest 96, 121, 125, 128, 138-139, 172, 201, 203-205, 242, 249
  postjudgment (interest) 204
  prejudgment (interest) 96, 201, 204
Joint Ownership Coverage Endorsement 49, 141-142
judgment 10, 31, 100, 203, 211, 224, 242
justified complaint 212-213

INDEX

law enforcement 247, 249
lawsuit 11, 80, 101, 105, 118-120, 125, 130, 150, 207, 209, 211, 246, 250
lawyer 11, 90, 120, 124, 127, 208-210, 245, 246, 248-250, 252
legal representative 80-81, 110
liability 2-3, 6, 9, 14, 16-17, 23, 25, 28, 30-32, 35, 38, 41-44, 48, 52, 64-65, 72, 79, 81, 83-84, 86, 89-130, 134-136, 141, 150-151, 163, 171, 174-175, 199-204, 208, 211-212, 217-218, 221-223, 225, 230, 240-241, 252
  bodily injury liability 2-3, 90-91, 108, 112, 114
  minimum liability 93
  personal liability umbrella policy 94
  property damage liability 2, 91, 171
liberalization clause 84
license 10, 25, 33, 104, 180, 186, 195, 232, 235, 240
  licensed drivers 5
lifestyle 22
limits of liability 41, 48, 92-94, 104, 111, 222
limousine 50, 217
line-item estimate 206
loss 3, 6, 11-18, 34, 41, 55-61, 63, 65, 69, 75, 77, 82, 84-85, 92, 108, 121, 135-140, 155, 159, 172, 174, 176, 180, 183, 196-200, 204-206, 208, 213, 218-221, 230, 243, 245-248
loss of consortium 108
Loss Payable Clause 138-139
lost wages 3, 18, 95
luxury car 34
malicious mischief 12
marital status 22-24
medical benefits 2-3, 127
medical expenses 6, 51-54, 98-101, 104-106, 108, 118, 123

Miscellaneous Type Vehicle Endorsement 42, 140, 142
model 25, 33, 35, 40-41, 125, 128, 130, 140, 178, 182-185, 200, 205, 211
  current model year 182-183
motorcycle 42, 53, 218
moving violations 25
multi-car risk 33, 35-36
named driver exclusion 85, 87
named insured 13, 39, 40, 45, 50, 72-74, 78-81, 108, 177, 234
National Highway Traffic Safety Administration 5
National Insurance Consumer Organization 149
negligent entrustment 234, 236
neighborhood 26-27, 177
net worth 28, 150, 222
no-fault 2, 9, 14, 51, 53, 85, 117-130, 250
  partial no-fault 120, 122-123, 126
  pure no-fault 119-122
non-owned auto 11-13, 45, 70, 198, 220, 222
non-renewal 178, 228-229, 233-234
non-standard risk 22
other insurance 64, 75, 94, 110, 111, 213, 217, 221, 230, 239
other than collision (OTC) 12, 25, 41, 42, 55-56, 70, 77, 85, 152, 162, 175, 205
out-of-pocket expenses 95
out-of-state coverage provisions 13, 95
ownership 49-50, 78, 106, 141-142, 173-174, 252
pain and suffering 3, 90, 95, 99, 121, 128-129, 173, 250
paper accidents 248
passengers 13, 16-17, 44, 49-52, 74, 119, 128, 141, 173, 217, 224
penalties 14, 30, 197

pension 29-31, 133, 134
personal accident insurance 17
Personal Auto Policy 11, 33, 41, 48-50, 55, 76, 91, 93, 104, 134-136, 140-141, 173, 217, 220, 222, 232
personal effects coverage 17, 76
personal injury protection (PIP) 53, 124-126, 128
personal-injury mills 248
phantom vehicle claims 248
pickup truck 49, 75
pleasure use 32, 187-188
points 9, 58, 146, 156, 165, 186-190, 246
police 184, 195, 197, 198, 220
policy 2-17, 21, 23, 26, 30-31, 36-49, 53-54, 56, 58-66, 69-101, 104-114, 118-119, 122, 123, 125, 128, 131-146, 156, 158-159, 164-165, 171, 174-175, 177-178, 186, 190-191, 193-194, 196, 198-199, 201-252
  policy limits 10, 94, 224-225
  policy number 39, 133
  policy period 40, 48, 61, 63-64, 70, 84, 141, 232
  policy provisions 132, 206, 212, 232, 242
  redundant policies 239
policyholder 6-7, 47-48, 54, 58, 71, 76, 82, 90, 101, 105, 122, 135, 140, 171, 175, 186, 201, 207, 209-210, 212-213, 215, 228-230, 243, 251
pre-existing duty 82
preferred provider option 147-148
premium 1-2, 11-12, 21-23, 27, 32, 34, 38, 40-44, 47, 55, 62-63, 70, 77, 81, 84-166, 170, 172-175, 178-180, 185-186, 190, 193, 201, 203-204, 216, 218, 222, 230-234, 239
principal operator 187-188, 190

pro rata 230, 231
proof-of-insurance card 194
Proposition 103 189
prospective loss costs 176
provisions 13, 61, 63-64, 75, 84, 87, 98, 100, 104, 111, 132, 174, 206, 212, 232-234
punitive award (punitive damages) 107
racing 88, 220
radar detectors 220
rate 1, 5, 7, 12-13, 15, 26-28, 30-31, 33, 35, 50, 54, 61, 66, 73, 85-88, 92-94, 99-101, 109, 114, 119, 126-129, 134-135, 137, 140, 142, 147-148, 154-158, 164, 166, 171-172, 174-185, 188-190, 195, 197, 209, 216-218, 222, 225, 231, 240, 242-244, 246-248
  base rate 27, 171, 175, 177, 181
  rate setting 7
  rating 6, 18, 23-24, 32, 58, 80, 129, 137, 171-178, 183-186, 189-190, 222
rating factors 22, 24, 185, 189
  primary factor (primary rating factor) 22, 24
  secondary factor (secondary rating factor) 24, 185, 189
  territorial rating 177
reasonable belief 65, 79, 110-111, 220
reckless driving 25
red-lining 26
reform laws 189
regulator 7, 117, 124, 207, 212, 229, 243, 251
regulatory trends 124
rehabilitation 2, 3
release 105, 203-204, 207, 223-224, 227-228
  enforcing releases 223
renewal 84, 180, 232-233

INDEX

rental car 3, 15, 16, 135, 196, 220, 248
repair 2, 59-60, 75, 77, 83, 90, 137, 140, 147-148, 153, 155, 163, 177, 183, 198, 200, 206
replacement insurance 10
replacement value 34, 42, 181
residence 76, 109, 128, 218
rights and obligations 47
riot 12
risk profile 22-23, 222
senior citizen 23, 166
service 3, 50, 75, 83, 145-148, 170, 212, 217
set-offs 97, 100
settlement 58-59, 66, 82, 120, 139, 140, 143, 160, 196-197, 199, 200, 205-206, 209, 210, 213, 215, 225, 235, 246-247, 249-250
single car risk 33, 35
sliding 239, 240
sound reproduction equipment 219
special interest groups 128
speed laws 220
speeding 25
split limits 27, 92-94, 134, 151
sports car 34-35, 156, 158
spouse 39, 45, 72-74, 80-81, 108
staged accidents 243, 248
stolen property 59, 60
sub-class 24, 185-186
subrogation 65-66, 82, 204-205, 221
supplemental liability insurance 17
suspension of insurance 133-134
swoop and squat 247-248
symbol 40-41, 181, 183-185
teenagers 25-26, 36, 157-159, 165, 179
telephone marketing 7
temporary substitute automobiles 13

INDEX

theft 2, 12, 16, 35, 60, 85, 88, 135, 138, 156, 159, 164-165, 177, 213, 223, 237, 245-248
threshold 118, 123, 250
tickets 165, 222, 228
time limitation 51
tort 91, 95, 128-129, 227
   limited tort coverage 95
   tort maintenance insurance 128
   tort reform 91
   tortfeasor 91
towing and labor costs 3, 38, 41, 155
traffic violations 165, 203, 233
umpire 61
underinsured motorist 3, 27, 35, 43, 53, 107, 113-114, 152
uninsured motorist 42, 44, 52, 97, 99-101, 103-105, 108, 110-111, 113, 115, 120, 128, 150, 151, 177, 198, 208, 224-226, 250, 252
vandalism 2, 12, 165
vehicle identification number (VIN) 25, 33, 37, 40, 70, 184
vehicle miles traveled 5
workers compensation 81, 97, 111, 216-217
young drivers 22, 36, 157, 188, 190
your covered auto 11, 12, 63, 65, 69, 78-79, 81, 84, 107-108, 110, 112, 140-141, 198
youthful operator 22-23, 177, 187, 190

20% OFF
MERRITT PUBLISHING BOOKS

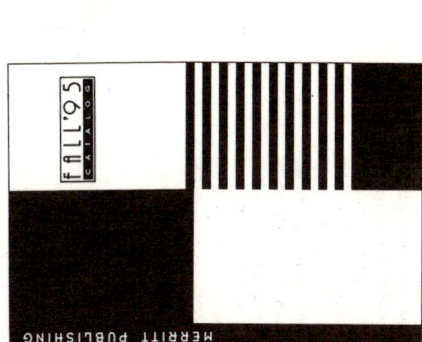

Merritt features a full line of books on key topics for today's smart consumers and small businesses. Times are changing fast – find out how our books can help keep you **ahead** of the times.

☐ **Yes!** Please send me a **FREE** Merritt Catalog, plus a 20% discount coupon good towards any purchase from the catalog.

Name _____

Company _____

Address _____

City _____ State _____ Zip _____

Phone _____

Merritt Publishing • Post Office Box 955 • Dept. SWAK • Santa Monica, CA 90406-0955 • **1-800-638-7597**   SWAK

SWAK

BUSINESS REPLY MAIL
FIRST-CLASS MAIL   PERMIT NO. 243   SANTA MONICA CA

POSTAGE WILL BE PAID BY ADDRESSEE

MERRITT PUBLISHING
POST OFFICE BOX 955
SANTA MONICA CA 90406-9943

NO POSTAGE
NECESSARY
IF MAILED
IN THE
UNITED STATES